FROM SOUTHAMPTON

Edited by Dave Thomas

First published in Great Britain in 2000 by
YOUNG WRITERS
Remus House,
Coltsfoot Drive,
Woodston,
Peterborough, PE2 9JX
Telephone (01733) 890066

HB ISBN 0 75431 848 6
SB ISBN 0 75431 849 4

FOREWORD

This year, the Young Writers' Future Voices competition proudly presents a showcase of the best poetic talent from over 42,000 up-and-coming writers nationwide.

Successful in continuing our aim of promoting writing and creativity in children, our regional anthologies give a vivid insight into the thoughts, emotions and experiences of today's younger generation, displaying their inventive writing in its originality.

The thought, effort, imagination and hard work put into each poem impressed us all and again the task of editing proved challenging due to the quality of entries received, but was nevertheless enjoyable. We hope you are as pleased as we are with the final selection and that you continue to enjoy *Future Voices From Southampton* for many years to come.

CONTENTS

The Poems

SITTING ON THE SIDEWALK

Sitting on the sidewalk keeping really still,
Looking to the darkness to a fox with her kill.
She's looking really graceful big and bold and proud
Moving like a predator still along the ground.
She's calling to her cubs saying the coast is clear
Looking at me sharply not showing any fear.
Five pairs of eyes full of dread looking at me coldly
Walking over to their mother, she's looking at me boldly.
They're playing really quietly in and out of the road
Ignoring their mother's warning calls, they're getting rather bold.
Their mother's going frantic on the sidewalk calling
They're looking to a pond not afraid of falling.
I can see the headlights of a car, I can hear the engine roaring
They're fed up with the pond, they're finding it quite boring.
Their mother's running to them in front of the moving car
It screeches on its brakes, a stench of burning tar.
She just makes it past the car and straight into a bush
Four cubs follow in quick pursuit, they all shove and push . . .
. . . Sitting on the sidewalk keeping really still
Looking to a fox cub that's just been killed

Kill your speed, not our wildlife!

Charlotte Slocombe (14)
Brookfield School

MY TRIP TO SINGAPORE

The fresh smell in the air
Sight of speeding cars
Up down in circles
Bump, bump, bump over the speed bumps
Sweet smell of coconut pineapple
On the grass the BBQ's going
Smiles as we meet family and friends
Going to smart places, Har-Par Villa, the dragon park
Fresh smell of leather
Hot sun shining
Excellent shops, Sony centres
Smells of curry, noodles and more
Buildings lit up as night falls
Music, dancing, singing
Three weeks later, home
Wishing we were still there.

Adam York (14)
Brookfield School

THIS IS THE TIME

This is the time,
When the creatures come to play,
This is the time,
When vampires come to slay.

This is the time,
When you can't go out at night,
This is the time,
When you'll get a horrible fright.

This is the time,
When the apocalypse is nigh,
This is the time,
When the human race must die.

This is the time . . .

Christopher Sharp (13)
Oaklands Community School

DRACULA

In the middle of the night,
A scary castle stood bolt upright,
Out he came all dressed in black,
Everyone called him old 'Count Drac'.
His sharp white teeth, and his long grey hair,
When you see him, he is such a scare.
I wanted to get out of this place soon,
As he looked at me from under the moon.
'What do you want?' I asked him there,
'Standing there with your long grey hair.'
As I said it he roared and roared,
And from that day I was his slave,
Scrubbing floors and windows too
Please come and rescue me very soon.
And from that day on I was working in pain,
Please come and take this pain away.
A year later I was there and said,
'Later I'll be lying in my coffin bed.'
I died in a terrible tragic way,
And I give this advice to any slave.
If he captures you and takes you in,
Try to break free and live within.

Becky Atwill (13)
Oaklands Community School

MY VIEW OF THINGS

I see my own world, in it are my things,
My hopes, dreams and wishes, land of loveliness.
Only visible to my eyes, my world is a crystal,
completely transparent.

You're invited into my world, but there's one catch,
you have to get there through my eyes,
See what I used to see, some sights may be
beautiful, some sights may be terrible.

Your eyes are the keys to unlocking your mind,
(they're not joking, when they say they can see
who you are through your eyes. Because it's true
they can).

Your eyes are responsible for any spectacular things
or horrible things you may see in your life.
The spectacular things are wonderful, a wedding,
a birthday or a new birth, are all special things.

Then there's the unhappiest moments you may view,
like someone being murdered or a kidnapping
anything that involves tears and sadness is
pretty upsetting too.

But just remember, I don't have my eyesight
and miss it every day, so much. Always value
your eyes, they're such a big part of your life.
Eyesight is precious and must be cherished, no
matter what.

Kylie Durand (14)
Oaklands Community School

IF GOD WAS A PERSON!

If God was a person,
That's if he was,
What would he look like?
The Wizard of Oz?

Or maybe Godzilla,
The king of the apes,
Would he run round like Batman
And wear silly capes?

Or even Bart Simpson,
Tarzan or Jane,
Would he be clever,
Or even insane?

If God was an animal,
Which would he choose,
The tiger or lion?
Which one couldn't lose?

If God had a name,
What would it be?
Terry, Peter,
Chuckie or Lee?

If God spoke a language,
Which one would it be?
German, French,
Or even Chinese?

All these answers,
I cannot see,
But what I'm certain of,
Is that God loves me!

Callum Dixon (13)
Oaklands Community School

KOMODO DRAGON'S SECRET

There is only one animal that I can think of that truly understands the meaning of life. Lots of animals seem to know but only one possesses the key to the unopened door that man has been searching for since the beginning of time.

For the reptilian creature of whom I speak is wise and learned with age, for he has been here since the dawn of the world. The reptilian creature of whom I praise is none other than the Komodo Dragon.

With his scales bouncing as if moving to a rhythmic beat with his head held high, proud and triumphant as he roams his domain. Then the people came and his life was once more threatened with extinction, but the Komodo Dragon is knowledgeable. He survived glaciers, meteorites and sandstorms. He would surely reveal a way to survive the humans. Before I finish this poem I will share with you the answer to the meaning of life, for the meaning of life is freedom, and freedom is never forgotten in the land of the
Komodo dragon.

Kristian Hill (13)
Oaklands Community School

THE FAMILY FROM HELL

First the mum is Winnie the Witch,
She throws naughty children into the ditch.
More horrible things are yet to come,
I wouldn't like her to be my mum!

Next the dad, a bloodsucking ghoul,
A freak, a failure, a definite fool.
He must be crazy, he must be mad,
I wouldn't like him to be my dad!

The first of the children, Warlock Wayne,
he specialises in causing pain.
He's much worse than his dreaded mother,
I wouldn't like him to be my brother!

The last of the children, a little wart,
She looks like an angel but is nothing of the sort.
She's a pig, a maggot, a little blister,
I wouldn't like her to be my sister!

What will happen? No one can tell,
This really is the family from hell!

Helen Cole (13)
Oaklands Community School

HALLOWE'EN NIGHT

Hallowe'en Night
Hallowe'en Night
All houses are lit
Everything is out of sight.
Hallowe'en Night
Hallowe'en Night
We're coming to your house
to give you a fright.
Hallowe'en Night
Hallowe'en Night
The streets are filled with darkness
and there is no light
Hallowe'en Night
Hallowe'en Night
The *trick or treating's* ended
The streets are now bright.

Hollie Green (12)
Oaklands Community School

WHAT IS A FRIEND . . . ?

A special friend is someone who
Will always keep in touch.
A special friend is almost like a sister
or a brother.
For there are things that you can
only tell to one another . . .
A special friend can help you through
your very hardest days,
or brighten up your good times with
their caring, thoughtful way.
That's why of all the many joys
that life could ever send,
There is no greater treasure than
a very special friend!

Shanna Cleary (12)
Oaklands Community School

SCHOOL (IS TOUGH!)

Lots of children,
in the playground,
after school it's homeward bound.
Handing out sweets,
behind the bike shed.
Kicking the ball at the teacher's head.
Jumping up and down,
on the skipping rope.
These poor teachers just can't cope.
'Stop that, Rita.'
'Cut it out, Jo!'
School is tough,
We both know!

Katy Frecknall (12)
Oaklands Community School

THE DRUNKEN MAN

I came across a drunken man
who'd had a little too much gin
he was knocking on a lamp post
and crying 'Let me in.'

'It's all a waste of time,' I said
'I'm sure there's no one there'
'There must be someone home' he said
'The light is on upstairs.'

I looked out of the window,
and saw the man still standing there
He looked up looking helpless
And I gave him a strong glare.

He then said to me 'Where do I live?'
I said to him 'How should I know'
He still stood there staring
I decided to give him a glow.

In the end I said
'I now don't care,
I don't like you
So why don't you stand over there?'

Arjun Malhotra (12)
Oaklands Community School

DOLPHIN

As the dolphin swims swiftly through the sea
She lives her life, just being free.
With the day in her head when things are going to change
She realises her life will never be the same.
The sound of the engine echoes in her head.
Frightened that soon she might be dead.
The drift net is like a mine box
When she cannot get out.
I wish that someone would hear her cry
Finally, when they do get caught,
Undignified tricks are now taught.

The human crowds can't wait to see
How intelligent these dolphins can be.

Michelle White (13)
Regents Park Girls' School

COSMETIC CRUELTY

L'Oreal and Vaseline
Test in ways which
Are mean.
We use them on our lips and
In our hair,
But we don't feel what animals
Bear.

Inject and burn to help
Scientists learn,
Animals want to live
But suffer and die
For our own selfish supply.

Buy products that are
Green,
Let's do a good deed
Stop the pain,
So animals are freed!

Ami Patel (14)
Regents Park Girls' School

SPRAY!

. . . Miserable, sad, lonely, deceived and cramped.
Sitting in a square-shaped cage; with bars made of rusting,
mouldy metal.
Life's getting shorter . . .
Sitting on the shelf opposite
is the dangerous can of sour deodorant; which will be sprayed
into the innocent and helpless eyes of the bunny
Life's getting shorter . . .
The horrible beast in the white, plain overall walking
towards the cage, the bunny
Whose heartbeat is getting faster,
louder
Stronger and then suddenly

Spraaaaaay!
The poor bunny whimpers loudly as its freedom is being
snatched away,
The poisonous substance is squirted meanly into its eyes,
The bunny struggling, bobbing round like a snake just
been whipped,
The bunny is screaming,
Terrified . . . !

Chetna Vaghela (13)
Regents Park Girls' School

ANIMAL POV

Imprisoned in a laboratory,
In a tiny cage,
I know my fate.
There's no escape.

Tomorrow they'll be testing,
Lotions, oils and cream,
They treat me like a Petri dish,
All I want is to be free.

Airless air and spaceless space,
Surround me in this tiny place
And I know I'll never see the light of day,
Again.

They'll torture me for days,
In many brutal ways.
They won't let me move,
So they can prove that,
All the lotions and creams,
Do not hurt the human beings.

But they are hurting me,
Can't they see?

They are hurting me!

Jessyca Eason (13)
Regents Park Girls' School

Fox Hunting

An exhausted fox runs in sheer agony,
Across open country,
Memories of freedom,
Fading away . . .

Hungry, bloodthirsty foxhounds,
Bare their teeth.
They increase their pace,
They are fitter than the fox.

As the fox runs his last few steps,
Memories of freedom,
fading away,
He hears the call of his fellow foxes,
Just whimpers on the horizon.

All of a sudden,
The fox feels sharp claws,
Gnashing teeth,
Attempting to rip him apart.

The fox's bones start to crumble
Like crackers,
His face turns red,
His eyes become cold.

The game of life is over for this fox,
But for the hunters,
It's just another day.

Kate McGrangle (13)
Regents Park Girls' School

CAPTURE

As free as a bird the dolphin swam through the billowing breeze
And whispering waves, so placid.
Not a care in the world, not a thought in its head,
Racing against the sunset.

The waves began to tremble like an earthquake hitting the sea.
A noise like thunder blasted over the quiet world,
The mechanical beast drew near.

The sound of muffled voices rang along the boat
The monster cornered the dolphin desperately swimming away.
A rattle of chains and it was over, the dolphin was trapped inside
Tangled up in the net, trying to get away.

They hauled up the precious load.
Motionless with fear, the dolphins' eyes were glazed to the
sea slowly disappearing.

Its loneliness was to begin.
The dolphin was tipped into a concrete pool.
It whimpered and cried like a child missing its family
As once it was taught to amuse,
Its wild nature abused.

As free as a bird, the dolphin once swam.

Louise Boswell (13)
Regents Park Girls' School

THE SEASONS

Summer shrivels into a
Chestnut shell,
While leaves start to rain down
In a shower of oranges, reds and browns.

Autumn rolls past,
Leaves and flowers shrivel fast,
As the cold wind whips the trees bare,
Until there's no life left visible.

Snow falls all around, while
Animals snuggle into hollows, nooks
And crannies.
Supplies of food everywhere.

Humans do the same,
Wrapping themselves up and
Huddling away from the bitter cold.
Stocked up with endless provisions of fuel and food.

Other than children's footprints
In the snow there's no sign of life,
No animals peeping out of holes,
Or scurrying away as you approach.

Nothing stirs,
Once the cold and frost sets in,
It's a struggle for all
Things to live.

Michelle Wallbridge (13)
Sholing Girls' School

MY CHRISTMAS POEM

December the 25th.
It's a very special day,
people are celebrating
in their own traditional way.

Children are excited
running about the place,
opening their presents
no time to waste.

The Christmas tree is glistening
pine needles everywhere,
no longer presents underneath
it really does look bare.

The family sit around the table
knives and forks in hand,
turkey, cranberry and Christmas pud
is served throughout the land.

The evening's packed with games and songs,
laughter brings many a tear.
What a shame this special day,
comes only once a year!

Rebecca Derwent (13)
Sholing Girls' School

JAKE'S ROOM

I really shouldn't be here, but
he's really not to know.
If I go very carefully, my presence
it won't show.
It's a risky business even stepping
into his room
My heart thuds quickly, searching
through the gloom.
Now a smell danger lurking
beneath the bed
Oh I was mistaken
smelly socks instead!
I put my hand on something,
it's given me a fright,
Oh my God, it's his pet spider,
squashed, it's dead all right.
Panic overtakes, I hear footsteps
at the door.
If I'm caught in here, I'll really get
what for.
Hiding now, breathing slowly, giggles
build up inside.
'What are you doing in my room?'
My brother Jake cries.
Full of rage and anger I see
my brother's face.
I've been told a hundred times,
Jake's room's a forbidden place.

Holly Bashford (13)
Sholing Girls' School

THE WOODS

Across the long road stood the bare woods,
The darkness and shadows beckoned every time she walked past,
Following her all along the road, like little prowlers.
A playground for children,
They weren't scared,
She always was.
Blotting out the sunlight, the trees hung over,
Whistling in the wind like a shrieking scream,
'No! You're imagining it!'
A shadow of a house in the distance,
Brown, black, thatched and frightening,
Guarded by the wood from who or what?
What were they trying to hide?
A secret?
A lie?
A mystery?

Emily Clark (14)
Sholing Girls' School

PETS!

My friend's dog is really mad,
sometimes he can be really bad.
He runs around and makes a riot
He never can be quiet.

My friend's hamster is really small,
She could be mistaken for a ball,
She always is asleep,
You can't even make a peep.

My friend's cat is really fat,
When she runs, she looks like a bat,
When she's out and about,
She doesn't look so stout.

Nichola Bolt (12)
Sholing Girls' School

ROMEO AND JULIET

A Montague fell in love with a Capulet,
The love of his life was Juliet,
But he had to follow his heart,
Because he didn't want them to drift apart,
Montagues and Capulets fought on different sides,
So they couldn't live together for the rest of their lives.
Romeo was so sad,
That he went running to his dad,
All Juliet wanted to do,
Was run away and have children with him too,
There was a big fight,
In the market last night,
With the Capulets and Montagues,
Lots of people died.
What a shame it was too.
Romeo made a decision,
And brought some roses with him,
He proposed that night,
She was full of delight,
They ran away together.
And lived happily for ever.

Kylie Baker (13)
Sholing Girls' School

FAMILIES

I have three little sisters,
One little brother,
My mum just told me she's having another.
My face went red,
My hair went grey
Can you imagine my feelings that day?
I dreaded to think,
I hated the thought
It's Dad, it's all his fault.
They're just like a plastic toy.
Could you imagine it, another thing,
When it's home and been born
I'll hate the thought,
Of its screaming - I'll yawn.

Joanne Gray (13)
Sholing Girls' School

CONTRADICTIONS

I was walking in the park
The sun was shining
It was dark.

It was warm 'cos it was May
But snow was falling
All the day.

I came across a wooden log
It was rolling in the grass
Turned out it barked, it was a dog.

Sam Smith (14)
Sholing Girls' School

HEALING POEM

I fell down and hit my head the other day,
I didn't think anyone would come my way.

But then a woman much older than me,
Came and knelt and held my knee.

She whispered softly to calm me down,
'Whatever happened? Did you fall down?'

I nodded my head and said 'Who are you?'
She smiled and said 'The name's Magoo.'

Then she said 'Where are you off to on this fine day?'
'I'm not sure,' I said 'I lost my way!'

'Where on Earth are you meant to be?'
'I'm meant to be going to meet Aunt Dee!'

'Oh' she said not knowing what to do,
'Perhaps you could use my phone, would that help you?'

I took the phone and she rubbed my head.
'When you get home, you should go right to bed!'

I dialled the numbers as she reached in her purse.
She pulled out a plaster, but I thought it was going to be worse.

As I spoke she placed it on my head,
I'm glad she was there or I'd be dead!

Georgina Spacagna (12)
Sholing Girls' School

MEDIA MOMENTS

From television to radio coming to our homes,
Faxes in the offices and busy telephones,
There's an underground network and wires above the roof,
Sending secret messages without any proof,
Jamming up airwaves,
Beaming out to space,
With all this technology, it's hard to keep apace,
Newspapers, letters, leaflets and notes,
Telling all who would listen to their stories and quotes,
Selling, telling, fibbing and lying,
Anything to attract you to buying,
Their words drawn from people and places,
People with sad, or some with happy faces,
We gulp down the words so carefully got,
Without a thought whether it be right or not.

Genna Goulty (14)
Sholing Girls' School

MY PAIN

The pain I have here,
I will keep locked up inside.
It's worth all my fear.
Even though I lied
Sometimes it appears
From deep down inside.
It comes out in tears
My hands feel tied
They've been there for years
I cannot hide all my fear inside.

Emily Farmery (13)
Sholing Girls' School

MILLENNIUM

What is the millennium?
1000 years.
What will happen?
How will things change?
Will there be robots which do our chores?
Will there be creatures with ginormous claws?
What's all the fuss with the Millennium Dome?
We know that soon it will be done and forgotten.
It's only an excuse to have a party bash,
Meet up with friends and family,
Buy tacky toys,
Singing funny tunes,
With big hats and shiny jackets.
Competitions going on
Who will have the best street party?
But one thing that must be asked
Is what will you be doing?

Freya Hillman (12)
Sholing Girls' School

CREEPY-CRAWLIES, SNAKES

Creepy-crawlies, snakes
Swimming in the lake,
Fear of creepy-crawlies
Turn out to be fake
Thinking they're alive
Kill them with knives,
Get those creepy-crawlies, snakes,
And draw them into my great big dirty lake!

Debra Bampton (13)
Sholing Girls' School

A PARTY ON MARS

It's a new millennium,
What shall I do?
I'll have a party,
You can come too!
We'll climb in a spaceship
And travel to Mars,
Won't it be great partying
In the stars.
Friends and aliens will
All be there,
Dancing and singing
Without a care.
People on Earth will never
Have seen such a sight,
The fireworks and light show
Will last all night!

Vikki Bartlett (12)
Sholing Girls' School

THE NIGHTMARE

I ran down the street as fast as I could,
My feet wouldn't stop I know that they should,
I heard footsteps behind me,
It must be a man,
It's dark and deceiving
. . . wake up Ann.

Becky Waters (13)
Sholing Girls' School

WHAT IS HEALING?

How can you heal a simple wound
Without knowing what to do?
Do I get help or do I get a plaster?
I want to help - tell people to 'boo hoo'
no more!
If you were to go to the Red Cross,
You could learn about how to help who,
And you'll never again forget -
Even St. John Ambulance will do.
You never know.
But to really help, you can comfort,
Be courageous, no one will mind.
Don't make a fuss and don't worry,
You only have to be kind,
Smile.
You can reassure, sympathise,
Give them a helping hand,
You might make a friend,
Don't slip, you don't know where you may land,
On something soft?
If they have medication, give them it.
Listen and understand,
Comfort and support them,
Bandage up their hand,
They won't mind.
Whatever you do, help them.
Get an ambulance, even better.
Doctors, operations - what matters?
Not even a thank you letter
Compared to life.

Elaine Aplin (12)
Sholing Girls' School

ROMEO AND JULIET

Romeo and Juliet
Montague and Capulet
Both in love with each other
One father did not like the other.

Romeo the Montague
Juliet the Capulet
Both in love
Their lives are woven.

Romeo and Juliet
Would not leave each other alone
I would dread to know
What would have happened if they had a phone.

They got married secretly
But it didn't grow happily
One night of bliss
Never had once a quarrel.

But sadly they both died
One drank poison
The other killed himself
With a knife.

Hayley Barnes (13)
Sholing Girls' School

LITTLE BROTHERS

Brothers, who would have them,
Certainly not me.
They get themselves into trouble
And put the blame on me.

They take your things without asking,
And hide them in their rooms.
They're horrible little monsters,
That should live on the moon.

Zoe Horn (12)
Sholing Girls' School

HAIR

Hair, hair,
It's everywhere
Over here and over there.
It's really unfair
When your head of hair
Makes everyone stare,
But their hair looks like a scary bear,
Some people care about their hair,
But some don't care
And their hair looks like a mare.
With my hair
I do what I dare,
Low or high in the air,
Sometimes I care
About my hair.
Some hair
Gives me a scare,
Some styles of hair
I would like to share.
In the end, hair's not that bad,
Some though, is a sight.
Now the big question -
What does yours look like?

Lauren Gibbons (12)
Sholing Girls' School

HEAL THE WORLD WE LIVE IN

We need to heal our world from war,
We need to show we care,
There are people who are poor,
Is that really fair?

Our world is filled with pollution,
It's mainly caused by us.
There is a simple solution,
Use the gas bus.

Heal our world we live in,
Heal it from pain,
Change it for our children,
Take away the shame.

Heal a friend from fear,
Assure them it's not true.
Tell them you are near,
If they're not sure of what to do.

Our world is full of people,
Homeless, ill and sad.
Some do not have enough to eat,
Why has our world turned bad?

Kayleigh Govier (12)
Sholing Girls' School

DREAMS

When you're fast asleep at night
And you're lying in your bed,
Images, thoughts and great creations
Creep inside your head.

Never in reality,
But always as a fantasy,
A whole new world inside my head.
Oh, how I love dreaming in my bed.

Louise Oliver (12)
Sholing Girls' School

FIRST DAY AT SCHOOL

Help! Help! I'm going to school,
Just keep very, very cool,
But what if I go wrong?
Then just sing a song,
But it's a big, scary school.

Do be quiet and go to school,
But I feel like a fool,
You're not a fool, you're a big baby,
I'm not. It's a big scary school.

You'll have fun.
Fun? Mum, shoot me with a gun.

We're here.
What! Take me home.

Go to school you will find a friend.
Maybe you're right,
Look, she looks like a good friend.

Leanne Mills (11)
Sholing Girls' School

IN A MUDDLE

The sun was shining and all was quiet,
Until I tripped over and made a riot.
My mum came quickly and asked what was the matter,
I said I felt as mad as a hatter.
She thought a little and took me home
And saw my leg was as big as the Millennium Dome,
She put it in a bandage and left it to heal
And that was about as much as I could feel.
I'm OK now apart from a lump,
but that's fine, because I'm hanging off of the washing line.
I feel like a bird, ducking and diving,
My lump has gone and I feel much better
And I only wish that I hadn't got so much wetter.
Of course you should realise that when I tripped, I fell
in a puddle,
That's what got me in such a muddle.

Lauren Miller (12)
Sholing Girls' School

WINTER WINDOW

Out of my window in winter
I can see
The naked, bare trees,
Just standing still,
Hear the whistle of the wind
Wrapping around the branches.
Then comes the snow,
So white, so soft, so peaceful,
The trees just sleeping in winter.

Polly Schoolcraft (12)
Sholing Girls' School

CAPITAL PUNISHMENT

I'm sat in my cell
wondering what to do,
I looked at my clock,
it's quarter to two.

In fourteen days
it's too late to try and mend
the terrible thing I did,
my life is going to end.

I know I shouldn't have shot her,
but what could I do?
She killed my wife
and tried to kill me too.

My mother always had a problem,
a problem with Jane,
said she wasn't normal,
she was insane.

She shouldn't have killed her,
that wasn't right,
so I killed her,
two deaths in one night.

So now I sit and wonder
in my smelly cell,
what death's going to be like,
when I go to hell.

Thanks for listening to me
before my time has come,
I'm going to be killed
for killing my mum.

Lucinda Lamont (13)
Sholing Girls' School

PUPPET DAY

The waiting silence stood quite still,
Until a sudden noise of thrill,
A wooden stick with lots of strings
On to the wooden stage they bring,
With beautiful colours and magical wings,
Across the stage but then a magical 'Ting',
The chiming of magic and moving so smooth,
I couldn't believe it, they moved with a groove,
From a few little things and a little egg box,
Along came the puppets, there were definitely lots.
They were made by the children of Sholing Girls' School,
But they looked so professional, like a Premier League ball.

Lynsey Withers (12)
Sholing Girls' School

WILD CATS

The murderous glare on their sly faces
as they hunt their prey
in the dead of night.
Their glowing eyes stay wide and bright
as they hunt their prey
in the dead of night.

That wonderful fur that imitates shadows
they use to blend in,
in the dead of night.
Their claws come out ready to fight,
fur that imitates shadows
in the dead of night.

They catch their prey, a well-deserved feast,
they share it around
in the dead of night.
They would never move or get a fright
as they eat their feast
in the dead of night.

Rhea Bawden (12)
Sholing Girls' School

WATERFALL

A waterfall shooting and darting off a wall,
as transparent as a crystal ball.

A fast runner winning a race,
shooting down a big hill.

Darting boxers crying with pain,
flowing down a stream.

Cantering horses jumping a wall,
like a bouncy ball.

A bird flying off a cliff.
Sparkling crystal on my face,
a swimmer rippling down a pool.

A dart flying for a bullseye.
A waterfall pouring off a mountain
made of rock.

A giant pool.

Lucy Newton (13)
Sholing Girls' School

Why The Whales Came

The Isles of Scilly sit in the sea,
their beauty and mystery is calling to me,
I set one foot on Samson and regretted it all my life,
my father said you cause me too much strife.
We knew it was the curse when my father disappeared
and all this time, this is what I had feared,
The Birdman had warned me his name is Woodcock,
he used to set sail from the big docks,
he would travel to Samson on his small boat
to light a small fire that was near a wet moat,
he then travelled back after the storm
and sat in the house to keep himself warm.
We ran to his house the very next day
to see him lying on the bay.
He had a big whale next to his side
that had very, very nearly died.
Everybody listened to the tale
of the night with the whale,
they helped push the whale in the water,
just before it nearly got slaughtered.
The very next day, everyone was sad,
something very good had turned into something bad,
the Birdman had died and so had the dad
of a very loving child and she wasn't glad.
Then all of a sudden, Gracie's dad appeared,
he said he had never even feared
when his ship had sunk he was dragged down,
'I didn't care,' he said with a frown.
Then Gracie knew the curse had been broken
when everybody had suddenly been awoken.

We all went to Samson that very day
to have a big picnic and to pray,
to hope that Samson would never be cursed,
but only ever be reversed.
So don't be afraid to find out the mysteries
of the great curse and the history.

Kerry Robertson (12)
Sholing Girls' School

THE WAY OF THE SEA

The sea starts off with a quiet sound,
Still and calm with nothing to be found.
In the sky, there's hardly a thing in sight,
It has been like this since last night.

In the distance you can see a boat,
And nearby something red afloat,
But all of a sudden it gets darker
And for the boat, it's making it harder.

Then the clouds start to come in,
Making the sky more and more dim,
And then the waves come on by,
It starts to rain so the waves get high.

Then the sounds on the sea are much louder,
In a few seconds it has got cloudier,
It sounds like a big drum banging,
Or even a bomb blowing.

Now the waves are roaring
And the rain is completely pouring,
But then it starts to get calmer,
And that's the way of the sea.

Kirsty Foreman (12)
Sholing Girls' School

THE HANGING

Rats scurried about her feet
And slime dripped down the wall,
Her death she was about to meet
In the county of Cornwall.

The death bell said its sermon,
Rattling keys unlocked the door,
Then a guard by the name of Herman
Yanked her off the floor.

The crowd all stopped and stared at her
As the cart bounced down the lane,
Her heart was pounding in her chest,
Soon never to be heard again.

The noose hung loosely in its cradle,
The crowd went deadly silent,
They pushed her up onto the platform,
Her death they wanted violent.

Her body was violently shaking,
Her hair in disarray,
The noose was slipped around her neck
To take her life away.

The bell was rung, the bucket kicked
The rope sank into her throat,
She felt her life being taken away,
She had no shred of hope.

And then it was all over,
Pain she felt no more,
The light engulfed her fragile body
And took her to Heaven's door.

Donna Ballan (13)
Sholing Girls' School

INNOCENT

The death bell rings,
There is silence all around,
The wind is still,
Nothing moves except for the rosary beads
Moving in his hands.
The executioner comes in dressed all in black
Then says to the man 'It is time.'
The man takes his last steps to the valley of death,
He is put in the chair and strapped in tight,
Even though he is upset, he does not put up a fight,
The executioner leaves the room to turn on the gas,
The gas seeps through the walls
And the man takes his last breath,
For something he did not do, the man is put to death!

Samantha White (13)
Sholing Girls' School

TEACHERS

Teachers, teachers,
Everywhere you go, there's always teachers,
Asking you questions about English and mathematics,
Chasing you up for your homework,
Hearing conversations that aren't anything to do with them,
or school,
Everyone's asking about homework, and there's you saying
you haven't done it.
Rushing here and there to get your work back.
School is quite busy here with teachers.

Victoria Marshall (12)
Sholing Girls' School

YOU'RE ALWAYS IN MY HEART

December is a very bad month,
I always seem to be down in the dumps,
Now you're in heaven watching us pray for you,
Missing all the things you used to do.
You've become an angel up above in the sky,
And then watching clouds going by.
Why did you leave us?
Why did you go?
Please tell me why, because I don't know.
I know you will watch over us until our time comes,
But till then I'll keep you in my heart always.
I love you dearly, but never showed you really.
I sometimes see you and Grandad too,
But don't worry Nan, I'll be right there with you.

Samantha Fullbrook (13)
Sholing Girls' School

CHRISTMAS

At Christmas, I get all excited,
In the morning I wake up early,
My sisters and I run into my mum and dad's room,
Screaming, 'Can we open our presents yet?'
Then we get even more excited, because
They say, 'Yes.'
When we have opened our presents,
We get really pleased because
We get exactly what we wanted.

Christie Slater (12)
Sholing Girls' School

MY LIFE

When I am in school, I will behave
And do all my work in lessons,
I will wear the right clothes
And do my homework for the day,
I will help the people around me
And when I am out of school,
I will do what I want
And have a lot of boys hanging around me.
I will behave like a lady, not a girl,
But when I am at home,
I will be in my room listening to my music.
When I am sad, I will be in my room
Listening to Backstreet Boys' 'As Long as You Love Me',
Because it makes me happy again.

Samantha Douglas (13)
Sholing Girls' School

THE WEIRDEST DREAM

In my dream,
I was walking on the beach
And I saw someone eating a peach,
Then I was in town
And I was dressed as a clown.
Then I ran to the park
And heard a dog bark.
When I woke up,
I had a hiccup and I said,
'No more cheese before bed.'

Hayley Dewey (13)
Sholing Girls' School

WHY CAN'T I BE PERFECT?

Why can't I be perfect?
Be someone really clean,
Be someone really patient,
Be someone with out greed,
Be someone really quiet,
Instead of really loud,
Someone really brainy
And make my mother proud,
Be someone who is sharing,
Be someone who's around,
Be someone big and better
To push little ones around,
Be someone really funny,
Be someone who is cool,
Be someone very different,
Maybe like you!
Not really!

Carly Webb (13)
Sholing Girls' School

1999

1999 what a wonderful year,
full of love and prosperity,
care and fear.

From the starving in Kosovo,
to the song, 'I'm Blue',
the Chinese year of the tiger,
what else is new?

Furbys were the toy of the year,
but in came the Millennium Babies
and now they're here.

The earthquake in Turkey,
in Devon an oil leak makes waters murky,
1999, what a wonderful year,
full of prosperity and fear.

Leah Manley (12)
Sholing Girls' School

ALIEN RUDE AWAKENING

I'm in my bed, wide awake,
It's half-past twelve,
It's dark outside in the wood.
I have to go to school in the morning,
I know I'm going to be in a bad mood.

Then I imagine aliens are coming.
I see a bright light,
The alien mother ship
Hovering above me
While I stand on the land.
I am amazed at what I can see,
Then I awake
With sweat running down my face.
It's morning
And it was just a dream . . .
Or was it?

Victoria Piatkiewicz (13)
Sholing Girls' School

MY DREAM

He enters, just standing there,
all dressed in black, almost like a cat.
He's skinny, not fat.

Sitting in the chair,
I come out from nowhere,
all my friends come in
looking dim.
They look at each other and remain silent.

He opens a bottle of gin,
he drinks the gin and puts it in the bin,
he touches my skin,
a rush of hate and love enters me,
what's going on here?
I walk towards my friends, then we laugh.

I wake up and it's a reminder of the other day,
from what my friends say,
it couldn't have been such a weird game
and it wasn't as bad as the play!

Laura Holloway (12)
Sholing Girls' School

THE RAIN

When the wind blows slow
And fast it sometimes carries rain,
But if it rains a little more,
You can tell that it is
going to rain for eternity.

Sarah Evans (13)
Sholing Girls' School

HALLOWE'EN

Never before have I felt so scared.
This thing came to the door, it was moaning and groaning,
The atmosphere was building up,
It looked so real - was it or not?
I screamed, my mum came rushing downstairs
In her Hallowe'en costume,
I told her and looked back
And it was *gone!*
That night I went to bed feeling very scared,
I found out the next day it was a ghost called George,
He died 150 years ago on Hallowe'en.
He got struck by lightning on the way to Mary's house,
The one he loved, who lived in this very house,
But only comes back on Hallowe'en.

Carri Jones (13)
Sholing Girls' School

BROTHERS

They get you into trouble,
When it's really not your fault,
Play tricks and take the mickey,
Yet rarely they get caught.
They nick all your belongings
And never give them back,
Agonise and tease you
So it's dignity they lack,
But if I think about it
From my brother's point of view,
He thinks the same of me,
As I do too!

Jessica Alsford (12)
Sholing Girls' School

SWAN!

There was a shiny silver swan,
Swimming smoothly south,
The water was just like a frozen mirror.

Their feathers were like silky satin,
Their beaks were yellow as the sun,
Their feet were webbed like dollies,
Their tails stuck out like a unicorn's horn.

Their nests are for their cygnets,
Their cygnets go squeak, squeak, squeak
When they're in their cuddly nests.
They looked like a grey man's head.

There was a shiny silver swan,
Swimming smoothly south,
They went with three,
And came back with seven swimming sideways.

Claire Adams (12)
Sholing Girls' School

LEAVES THAT BLEW

There once was a leaf, nice and green,
Sitting on the treetop where it should be.
It soon came down though in a breezy wind,
And landed on a nice soft green.
It turned yellow and brow in the crisp winter sun,
To then disappear in the greenkeeper's drum.

Natasha Lloyd (13)
Sholing Girls' School

IN THE SUMMERTIME

In the summertime when it's always hot,
Children run around getting people wet,
Playing in their pools, cooling down,
Licking their lollies, yum, yum, yum.
Going to the beach, splashing around,
Making sandcastles with a moat,
Standing in the shade, hiding from the sun,
At the end of the day, we have had loads of fun.
Going back to school with our lovely tans,
Talking with our friends about the holidays,
Some people go to other countries and
Away from roads and noise,
But I like a holiday with my friends here at home,
Splashing about.

Charlene Smith (13)
Sholing Girls' School

SEA STORM

The clouds start rolling over the sun,
Taking the light and making it glum.
The waves start creeping up to the shore,
Higher and higher up to the sky they bore,
Crashing down and whipping up,
Swirling and banging against the rocks,
The rain tumbles down into the sea,
Whilst the white foam rushes around,
The wind swerves angry and mad
The water's spray fly in the air,
Lightning and thunder boom and shake,
Until the clouds move away
And the sea returns to a gentle sway.

Nichola Mole (13)
Sholing Girls' School

ANIMALS

There's the rabbit in the forest,
Hopping at his fastest
Because he's being chased by a fox,
Faster and faster does he hop.

Cats are running from gardens,
Faster and faster, running and running.
When he finally gets home,
Around the house he walks.

In the forest there's a deer,
There's only one thing they fear.
It's the lion that is feared,
The lion will eat it if it's heard.

The cheetah runs everywhere,
Climbing trees here and there,
Whatever they want to eat,
They will catch it 'cause they cheat.

Marie Ballard (12)
Sholing Girls' School

HALLOWE'EN

Hallowe'en is here at last,
Sweets, tricks and fun for everyone.
Children going door to door saying 'Trick or treat.'
Witches, ghosts and ghouls,
Are they real, or just for fun?
Midnight is near, so all beware
Those not at home do not live to see next year!

Jodie Sillence (13)
Sholing Girls' School

CHRISTMAS DAY

Reindeer in the sky,
pulling along the sledge,
Santa delivering presents
stacked at the foot of the bed.

It's very dark
as I creep down the stairs,
flick on the light switch,
Wow! Presents everywhere.

Some very large ones,
some funny shaped ones,
lots with ribbons and bows,
all of them stacked right under my nose.

Opening all of my presents
to see what's inside,
is it what I asked for,
or is it a surprise?

I've left the biggest till last,
the heaviest one of all.
I wonder what's inside?
A computer would top it all!

I've got to have my breakfast now,
Mum says I'll have to wait,
I want to open my present,
but I guess I'll just have to wait.

I've now been sent to the bathroom
to wash my hands and face,
to brush my teeth and look my best
and hopefully, not a disgrace.

Hayley Whitlock (11)
Sholing Girls' School

CHRISTMAS AT LAST

It's Christmas Day,
We start to pray
To see what presents make my day.
It's Christmas at last!

Wake up quick
To see Santa's trick,
I run downstairs in a tick.
It's Christmas at last!

I banged open the door,
To bang what's on the floor,
Surprises, surprises all round the door.
It's Christmas at last!

I tear off the wrapping paper
And shout 'Eureka!'
It's Christmas at last!

One to go, but not the last,
It's massive, it's huge,
It's so heavy I can hardly lift it.
It's Christmas at last!

I tear it, I open it
And . . . *woof!*
It's a baby puppy.
Doh! Christmas is nearly over

Hazel Upson (11)
Sholing Girls' School

THE DAY

The sun is shining,
Twinkling bright,
With skipping girls singing nursery rhymes,
The sun still climbs.

It shines on the fields of golden buttercups,
Bringing forth
The forever busy bee,
Gathering pollen for my tea.

I lie under a tree
And slowly drift and dream
Of bread and honey,
Golden and smooth.

The sun is glowing,
The shadows are growing,
Skipping ropes are slowing,
The day is slipping.

The moon is taking over
With twinkling stars,
To watch the girls as they snuggle in their beds,
With heads full of rhymes and happy times,
And other days.

Alison Marshall (13)
Sholing Girls' School

WHAT IS IT ABOUT RAINBOWS?

Why does the rainbow shine so bright
And how come the rainbow doesn't shine at night?
Is it a secret about the pot of gold?
If so how come this secret is never told?
There are seven colours in the rainbow
But there is no white as bright as snow!
There is no black as dark as the midnight sky,
And how come you can't reach the rainbow even if you fly.
What causes a rainbow?
Why don't I know?
Is it because the sky wants to smile?
Its smile so big, it's as long as a mile!
Can rainbows see like you and me?
Can rainbows talk or can they walk?
Is a rainbow friendly, kind and keen
Or perhaps it's nasty, cruel and mean.

Why are there so many questions to answer
About the mysterious rainbow?

Shelley Flaherty (12)
Sholing Girls' School

CATS

Cats are funny,
Cats are sweet,
You should see a cat
When it's got a piece of meat.

Kayleigh Maidment (13)
Sholing Girls' School

FRIENDS

Friends can be so annoying,
and really have got a nerve,
but sometimes they can be so nice,
you can tell them secrets and they won't
say a word.
My best friend is just like this,
we split up the other day you see,
but when we made up, it was like we never broke up,
but I guess that's the way it's got to be.

It all started the other day,
when we were out on our bikes.
Her bike skidded out of control,
I didn't mean for a fight.

I burst out laughing
as she flew through the air,
she got so angry
she went up like a flare.

She limped away
as I ran after her,
she said she never wanted to see me
for ever and ever.

That night when I lay
in my bed,
I though about the dreadful things
she and I said.

So the very next day
I rang her up,
we both said sorry,
laughed and made up.

Caroline Ashdown (12)
Sholing Girls' School

THE UNICORN

Galloping swiftly through the night,
Her mane shimmering as white as the moonlight.
Destination? I know not where,
But she will keep going until she gets there.

Bleak white snow describes her hair,
She is so very beautiful, this mare.
Her horn is as clear as a crystal tip,
Don't worry, she won't bite, she'll just nip.

Running, running on and on,
Keep on going, the battle is nearly won.
Passing through clouds and sunbeams,
She's also passing through children's dreams.

Her journey is finally complete,
Finally, at last it's done,
Her battle is now won,
She will now come into my dream,
And then start a journey on a new sunbeam.

Natasha Carr (12)
Sholing Girls' School

WINTER

When the winter starts to unfold,
everybody catches a cold.
The rain is pouring,
the snow is falling
and people are feeling down.
The children are behaving,
'cause Christmas is coming
and Santa is coming to town.

Christmas is here,
the children shout and cheer,
Santa has left some surprises,
there are all different shapes and sizes.
Families are playing games,
some people win,
the countdown to the millennium will soon begin.

Michelle England (12)
Sholing Girls' School

TO ME

To me you are an angel,
You shine just like a star,
To me the heavens open up,
When I see you just how you are.

To me you are the funniest person
That I have ever known,
Every single thing you do
Brings out the happiness in me, from you.

To me everything you do is right,
You are my sunshine, my only light.

To me you are always kind,
When I am lonely, sad or ill
You take care of me.
To others you are just the same,
But in a much more helpful way.

To me you are a friend indeed, you really are my chum.
When I look closely, deep inside I know still, you are my mum.

Rorie Byles (12)
Sholing Girls' School

FROGS

Jumping up,
Jumping down on a lily pad,
They are green or maybe brown,
Try to catch them if you can.

Jump and hop,
Do the froggy dance,
Find the biggest lily pad
And put it in a pond.

Pay a pound
To see a queen,
'Cause I've got the most beautiful frog
You've ever seen.

Claire King (12)
Sholing Girls' School

DAY

Day is good, it is light,
It makes me feel very bright,
I am always happy when the sun shines,
I will not moan or ever groan.

When night comes, it is my nightmare,
It makes my wicked side appear,
I'm not a werewolf though you might think,
I'm just a little girl who doesn't sleep a wink.

Day is good, it is light,
It makes me feel very bright.
It makes me shine like a light,
The brightest you've ever seen.

Chelsey Weeks (12)
Sholing Girls' School

THE SUNSET

The sun is setting
Over the hills.
It's really calm and relaxing.
The animals go in from playing
Because it's getting darker,
The day is going home.

The sun is like
A fire's glow,
Hot red, warmly orange, cold yellow
Takes over the evening sky.

The sun has set,
It's time to go,
Until tomorrow when it's 7.30am
When the sun rises in the morning sky.

Deborah Kingston (12)
Sholing Girls' School

WEATHER

Windy air, cold air,
Everywhere around me,
Another day comes,
Together we can make it warm,
Here together we can make the weather change.
Every time I can hear rain,
Really another rainy day comes,
But I still love the weather.

Claire Rustell (13)
Sholing Girls' School

HALLOWE'EN SPOOKS!

The time has come when Hallowe'en is here,
Tricks, treats and all things we fear.

Black cats and witches' hats,
Ghosts, zombies and all of that.

Costumes, disguises, masks
And surprises.

Cauldrons bubbling with poison potion,
That will set your heart in a racing motion.

Creepy-crawlies and fluttering bats across the blood-red sky,
Makes you hungry for pumpkin pie.

Vampires, fangs and frightening clangs,
Ends the Hallowe'en and leads us to the November bangs.

Emily Roberts (12)
Sholing Girls' School

CATS

Cats are on the window,
Cats are on the floor,
Cats are in the kitchen,
Cats are in the hall.
Biscuits, biscuits,
More, more, more,
Biscuits, biscuits,
Or we will knock down your door.

Lisa Sheath (13)
Sholing Girls' School

BLUE CROSS CAT!

A naughty little black and white kitten
Lives in my house in the middle of Bitterne.
She's not a dog, and won't do as she's told,
She'll end up at Blue Cross before she gets old.

Her sharp little teeth draw blood when she bites,
When I let her outside, she gets into fights,
She scratches the walls and misses her litter,
She'll end up at Blue Cross if she doesn't do better.

Hairballs in corners, sick on the mat,
Mum's had enough of this terrible cat,
I loved her so much, but it's time to say goodbye,
She ended up at Blue Cross and I wanted to cry.

Sam Harper (12)
Sholing Girls' School

MATHS

I find maths easy,
but difficult at times.
Some of my friends don't like it
as much as I do.

I'm sitting down in my chair,
my brain is working hard,
I'm trying to work out the answers,
my brain is stretching, I can feel it.

The bell rings,
I haven't finished.
We hand our books in
and I silently walk out.

Charlotte Gurd (12)
Sholing Girls' School

HALLOWE'EN!

On an enchanting night,
When the moon was alight,
The ghouls and ghosts
Came out to play.

When the little children
Dressed as wicked witches,
And gross, gory ghosts,
The pumpkin's face glares at you.

It's the devil's night to play with your minds
And make you want to run and hide,
The goblins chase the fairies,
Then the night gets started.

The gruesome grizzlies came out
And the spooky, spine-chilling scarecrow
Makes his entrance,
Only keeping one promise,
that is to eat little children.

Galloping across the horizon
When dawn is about to fall,
The skeleton rider decides to top it up,
He looks at you with his red eyes.

Don't go where, don't go where,
Don't go where the ghouls are,
Don't go where, don't go where,
Don't go, don't go.

Heather Cole (12)
Sholing Girls' School

FIREWORKS

The fifth of November,
The fifth of November,
Another firework night to remember.
The roar of the fire,
The smell of the gunpowder,
The rockets go higher,
The explosions get louder.
They whoosh up, they sparkle,
They light up the skies,
The joy of the crowd can be seen
In their eyes.
The rockets go up,
Then they fall to the ground,
The patterns they make can be seen all around.
The sparklers sprinkle in the air,
And children enjoy them everywhere.
Also at my firework night
We had a Guy Fawkes man,
We thought he looked like a young English boy
So we eventually called him Sam.
I can't believe my firework night is over,
The fire has now gone down till the last ember,
A new day awaits,
The sixth of November!

Rebecca Gibbs (12)
Sholing Girls' School

I Wish

I wish I was a bird,
I could fly away into the clouds,
Whistle a happy tune.

I wish I was a fish
Swimming in the sea,
I will be so free.

I wish I was a mouse
I'd scuttle and I'd hurry
I would be so sneaky and quiet.

I wish I was a snake
I would slither, I would hiss,
I would sunbathe all day long.

I wish I was a horse
Galloping through the countryside,
Laying on the grass.

Sometimes I wish
What I can't be
Because I am me.

Lianne Birkett (14)
Sholing Girls' School

A Stormy Day

Clouds fly over and cover the sun,
The wind howls as the thudding rain pours,
The thunder bangs like a drum.
The lightning flashes and crashes like a sea storm.

Then all of a sudden the lightning calms down
And the thunder slowly stops banging,
As the thudding drops of rain turn to drips
And the clouds uncover the sun.

Heidi Spranklin (13)
Sholing Girls' School

THE ANGRY MAN

There was an angry man
Who was never nice,
Once he had a wife
But still was not nice,
One day he brought a dog,
Can you guess? Yes he was still not nice,
Then he started to think about being nice.
In the end he said sorry to his wife,
She said don't worry.

So now he was always nice
And always got rice,
Now his wife is always nice
And cooks him rice,
The dog now likes his bone
Because the man has a nice tone,
He thinks he's cool
'Cause now he's nice and he's tall.
He tries very hard to be nice.
Every time he goes to be horrible
He says I'm sorry.

Victoria Shirley (11)
Sholing Girls' School

THE SUNSET

The sunset, a mixture
of pink and orange.
The sun peeking up over
the hills.

The sea calmly swaying
back and forth,
The fishermen go fishing at sunset,
The kids come and play before it gets dark.

When the sun goes down
And the kids go in,
It goes quiet,
Then you stand up and look out to sea.

The cold air whooshes in my face,
A cold feeling comes over me.
Then the dolphins swim towards
The waves and play about.

Perhaps this will not end,
Maybe it will,
I . . . just . . . don't . . . know.
But we know for sure that nothing
can
beat
the
sunset.

Jenna Moger (13)
Sholing Girls' School

AS TIME PASSES

I sit and willingly watch
from the window of mine.
The atmosphere is quiet and divine
As I turn to my watch I can see it's the time.

When the squawking seagulls
fly fitfully down upon the sea's waves,
Begin searching like pickpockets,
You would have thought, they hadn't eaten in days.

As the time passes
The seagulls fly away.
But I can be sure,
They'll be back another day.

As the morning begins to get lighter,
The fishermen come into sight.
Trawling for their daily trade,
Catching fish from day till night.

It is all like a competition,
All sorts of nets being thrown into the sea.
All of them fearful, fighting fish,
I'm sure glad it's not me.

So this is what happens,
On a regular day.
Always the same,
As I look out on the bay.

Olivia Back (12)
Sholing Girls' School

IN THE KITCHEN

My mum was cooking
and my dad was looking
for my fluffy cat, Mall
who was sitting on the wall.

The dog was barking
and my brothers were fighting.
and they were rushing about
like lightning.

They tripped up Mum
and she dropped her pan,
and my brother skidded
on the floor.

He knocked over Dad
who went absolutely mad,
it was quite a day we had.

Chloe Turnbull (12)
Sholing Girls' School

THE DEATH OF TIME

Silence reigns as the death toll rings,
The clock begins to tick,
Footsteps pounding down the hall,
The man begins to feel sick.
The drums are beating in his head,
Quickens does the clock,
It won't be long before he's dead,
Just as soon as death knocks.

Kayley Garner (13)
Sholing Girls' School

IN THIS DARK AND GLOOMY LIFE

I feel locked up like an animal,
An animal in a cage.
I'm forbidden to do anything and
I'm forced to do chores and I'm
Not even allowed to watch TV.
TV what is TV?
What does it do?
How does it work?
What does this gloomy plastic box do?
Why am I treated this way?
Why can't the people who I slave for love me?
Who am I and how did I get here?
What is love?
Does love spare my name in its course?
I guess not, it's just something that comes and
Goes as it pleases, like me!
I wonder if I'll ever be loved and see love the way
I want it to be in this dark and gloomy life.

Claire Handley (14)
Sholing Girls' School

POEM ABOUT PEOPLE WHO BLAME THE FAULTS OF THEIR FEET ON THEIR SOCKS

Smelly, smelly, smelly socks,
Why do they smell so much?
I've washed them once, I've washed them twice
But then the smell is still left behind.
Smelly, smelly, pongy socks.
Then I ask 'Whose feet have been in these?'
Then I remember it was my *daddy's cheesy feet!*

Kelly McCormick (12)
Sholing Girls' School

FORGOTTEN

Rigor mortis takes over feeding on death
Skin is candlewax dripped
Forming cold pallor
Eyes transfixed on an unseen object
Cradled within a velvet box.

Bedroom of darkness
Must and damp seep within its walls
Cadaver feeds a thousand ravenous beasts
They sit and eat their fill
Leaving behind rancid remains.

Skid laden with dents
Putrid rotten flesh, leaves behind
A suffocating stench that fills the tomb
Nicotine stained fingers of bone grip the air
With hands that pray for another chance.

All memory of life diminshes
Vanishes with its outer shell
While all that is left behind is the frame
And a stone that speaks of its existence
But that too fades in time all is forgotten.

Becky Winkworth (14)
Sholing Girls' School

THE WIND

Whirling, dazzling, swirling around,
An invisible force that no one can
See - but everyone knows it's there
And blows your skirts up in the air.

Lyndsey Strong (12)
Sholing Girls' School

MY TRIP TO TITCHFIELD!

It was rainy
But just for us.
We travelled there
On a bus.

When we got there
We had our lunch
But during the trip
We still had a munch.

Our work was ruined
By the rain
And in the end
It became a real pain.

We walked around Titchfield
To do our research.
Lucy lost her camera
So we all did a search.

We went to the river
To do a quick sketch
But then in the end
Our paper was too wet.

Then the time was 3 o'clock,
We all had to go back to the bus.
So we all had to stop
Because there it was waiting for us.

When the bus stopped
We were back at school.
Everyone got their things
And went into the hall.

Preciana Fernandes (12)
Sholing Girls' School

FIRE IS A HUNGRY LION

Fire is a hungry lion,
Chasing his prey.
A king they say,
When he feeds himself he grows,
So large, so loud, so long,
He runs so fast he cannot stop,
He springs so high he hardly drops.

Hour by hour he stalks the land,
Growing large, larger than man can.
He kills, he howls, he moans,
Through the night all different tones.

But soon he dies no more to roar,
He makes no sound,
Doesn't move any paw.
His life is over, no oxygen to breathe,
The fire is out, now the kingdom grieves.

Jennifer Edmonds (14)
Sholing Girls' School

FROGS

Frogs are small
And never tall.
They hop around
And touch the ground.

They make a sound,
There are other frogs around.
They sing so cool
People think they're fools.

They go to sleep on lilies,
That might sound silly.
Frogs are small
And never tall.

Lisa Bevan (12)
Sholing Girls' School

FAMILY

F   un to be with
       friends all around
       fights not too many.
A   lways there
       to discuss
       to laugh
       to comfort.
M   um to cook
       mum to wash and iron
       me to help
I   am individual
       I am me, but only because
       of my family
L   oving family is what you need
       lots of fun and hugs
       learning all the time
Y   oung and old mixing well
       you're all thrown together
       yes, the family is where it's at.

Katherine Ward (14)
Sholing Girls' School

DREAMS

I have a dream
That one day I will fly like a bird.
Stand up for my rights,
And make myself heard.

I have a dream
That everybody is treated alike.
All animals live,
Like dodos, whales and pike.

I have a dream
That oil does not exist,
And nor does pollution,
Or litter, on goes the list.

I have a dream
That snakes will keep their skin,
Mink would keep their fur,
And hyenas would keep their cheeky grin.

I have a dream
That recycling bins were number 1,
And so were bottle banks,
Dropping litter would not be done.

I have a dream
That trees were left still standing,
And would not hit the ground
With a terrible landing.

I have a dream
That giant pandas were free to roam.
And children are warm and dry,
And had a friendly family and home.

I have a dream . . .

Lucy Kingdom (12)
Sholing Girls' School

STRUCK BY FEAR

The clouds part away from the moon,
It's like time doesn't seem to pass at all,
The silk light lays a misty gloom,
You feel alone, no one can hear you call.

People fight like there's no tomorrow,
Deep black thoughts invade their minds,
Seeing friends die can bring such sorrow,
Fear of man can turn one blind.

What seemed like a dream turned to death and dying,
The sound of guns and people crying,
But who can help the injured and save another life?
Who can help the injured and risk another life?

Who will dare to cross the space
Where people lay without a breath?
Who will dare to cross the place
Where death is danger and danger is death?

Nothing can change the faces of fear,
This case of judgement in court won't hold,
A trial of war has no existence here,
History is a story just waiting to be told.

Danielle Young (15)
Sholing Girls' School

WHO NEEDS LOVE?

Love, who needs love?
As you grow older the word becomes a completely different issue.
Whenever you really need someone, that is when love strikes.
When you cry for them day and night,
Who you permanently talk about when you're down,
Their name is plastered in your mind.
You can't help the day you fall in love,
The excitement, the thrill and the anxiety,
As you walk side by side in the fresh morning dew.
The situation doesn't matter,
As long as you're with them.
Sometimes you can't understand why you love someone so much,
And sometimes you never do find out until they are gone.
Your love turns into a heartache,
Which no one can explain.
Love is like a pink rose,
So gentle, smooth and delicate.
But when the season is over
It changes back into a bud.
You'll never know the secrets you always thought you knew,
So who needs love anyway,
Those famous words, 'I do'.

Claire Holmes (15)
Sholing Girls' School

MY FAVOURITE GUINEA PIGS

I go out to the shed in the morning,
And I hear both of my guinea pigs calling.
They sit in their hutch squeaking for a treat,
Carrots, tomatoes, just vegetables no meat.

But when I'm at school they wait all day,
Just lay on their tummies munching on hay.
But when I get home I put them straight in their run,
So they can munch on grass and have lots of fun.

Kathryn Grubb (11)
Sholing Girls' School

LOVE

Imagine love as a flower,
Growing and changing,
The sun comes out dawning a new day,
Intoxicating you, like a drug,
Getting under your skin, in your veins and
pumping through your heart,
You succumb to its intense powers,
Opening your petals and inviting it in,
But the weather never stays the same,
Grey skies clutter your vision,
It's inevitable that rain is on its way,
One drop then another falling from everywhere
like soldiers on a mission,
Aiming their heavy bodies onto your delicate petals,
You keep praying for them to stop,
But they just keep on more and more and more,
It's funny sometimes how love can feel so lonely,
Standing out there in that big empty field unable to run away,
Waiting patiently, loyally for the sun to come out again.

Halima Ottway (15)
Sholing Girls' School

WITCH'S POTION

Devil's fork,
Old dead hawk,
Snail's shell,
Toilet smell,
Frog's leg,
Smelly cracked egg,
Rattlesnake's tail
And cold hail,
Add some stones,
Dead man's moans,
Slimy slug,
And some mud,
Dead rats,
And mashed up cats,
Bibble, bubble, smell trouble,
Hubble, bubble that's the spell,
Here's the witch, let's run, run, run.

Elizabeth Thomas (11)
Sholing Girls' School

HALLOWE'EN

I walk into a haunted house,
There I saw a mouse.
Scary ghosts and bats and witches
with strange hats,
And pumpkins everywhere.
I ran out and dropped my sweets
so I had to get more treats.
My Hallowe'en was very exciting
but it was very frightening.

Kelly Green (12)
Sholing Girls' School

WHEN I STARTED SECONDARY SCHOOL

When I started secondary school
I felt cool.
When I had PE,
I then had RE.

You can play ball,
only in the hall.
I care for my friends,
they're my responsibility.

Get everything packed away
and this is your way.
We care
if you care.

Jessica Butt (12)
Sholing Girls' School

PRANCE

She darts around and swats in the air,
Then looks confused when nothing's there.
Pick her up and pet her soft fur,
Listen closely, and you'll hear her purr!

She is a loveable cat,
Cute as can be,
Now put her down and
Let her sleep.

She comes up to say, 'Hello!'
Then she goes back down below.

Zara-Jane O'Rourke (12)
Sholing Girls' School

THE FOOTBALL MATCH

I can hear the noise of the crowd echoing in my ears,
The smell of the burger stand, hot dogs linger in the air.
The sky above is grey with cloud
But the commentary is clear and loud.
On the pitch in front of me playing dive and weave, in the
                                box the keeper's ready,
In comes the cross nice and steady.
Here comes the quick kick,
It flies past the goalie.
The game's almost over,
The whistle blows,
The crowd slowly goes.
I leave the ground and lose the adrenaline,
My breathing is normal but my throat is *aching!*

Louise Dean (12)
Sholing Girls' School

CHRISTMAS

Children, children, the mothers say oh look it's presents.
Saint, Saint thank you for this present.
Oh why, oh why is there no snow,
I, I really enjoy the snow.
Oh, oh what a wonderful Christmas tree and a
Brilliant day that's because it's Christmas.

So, so close your little tiny eyes,
Don't, don't open them or you'll spoil your surprise.
Christmas is fun.

Charlotte Currie (11)
Sholing Girls' School

CHRISTMAS IN THE TRENCHES

It's been a year since it first started,
Everyone's learning to be strong.
We thought the Germans were cold-hearted,
Now we realise we were wrong.

It was the Christmas of 1914,
And everything was dead,
Then we saw the glowing light,
Shining from ahead.

We shouted at each other
For the war to end,
We met right in the middle
And saluted to the men.

We had a Christmas football match,
The Germans won 3-2.
We traded gifts and presents
So we had things that were new.

We had a burial service,
Not as two but one.
Shots were fired in the sky
From the Captain's gun.

The war had started up again
And everything was loud.
All I saw was firing
From the German crowd.

Emily Pattimore (15)
Sholing Girls' School

CHRISTMASTME

Green land to white land while snows fall,
Dinners being cooked inside the big brick wall.
It's dark outside,
Snow covers the slide.
The children hang the stockings up high
Just above the big mince pie.
A glass of milk like the snow
And above the fire two bits of mistletoe.
Santa comes with an almighty crash,
The children are woken by the big loud bash.
Up and around the great big house,
Down the stairs to find a very small mouse.
He looks up and squeaks
Then runs away, Mum won't dare to have a peek.
5.00am back to your beds,
Fill those very small heads
With sugar and candy toys and joy
While Mum called Mandy to tell her about the boys.
In the morning sacks are full,
Stockings are falling off the wall.
Bright red bows tied up tight
While the Christmas fairy is afraid of heights.

Amie Watts (11)
Sholing Girls' School

FRIENDSHIP MEANS NOTHING

Friendship means nothing,
Nothing, nothing at all.
Friends stink,
Friends who needs them?
Not me.

Friends get you into trouble,
Friends get you into fights.
I see friends playing rough,
I see friends fighting,
I see friends falling out,
That's why friendship
Means nothing to me.

Cherrie-Lea Holman (11)
Sholing Girls' School

THE FOX OF SPRINGTIME'S DEW

(This poem was written in honour of everyone who has
sacrificed all to save others and to give us the freedom of
speech no matter what the consequences may be.)

The fox of springtime's dew drops glistens in the sunlight.
Looking forth on the other animals awakened from their winter
slumber by him on his morning prowl.

He barks at winter's fingers, he plays with springtime's cubs, he
loves all around him as he's the springtime's fox.
His own cubs are Hunnysuckle, Tulip and Autumn.
Their names tell all of what they will be.

His fire red tail, bushy like a fleece covers all who sleep within
his reach keeping the Queen of the North at bay.

With his paw half raised surveys the landscape surrounding him
keeping us all safe, yet free to be whom we want to be.

Forever and a day he will do this. From the depths of his grave,
from his cloud in the sky above, to his own home he will always
be with us.

Gemma Rooke (15)
Sholing Girls' School

SCARED

One morning I was awoken by the sound of people screaming,
I felt dazed and didn't know what was going on,
Why were they screaming? Why were people peering
Out of their windows? What was going on?

I looked out of my window too and was very shocked
To see buildings on fire and hearing loud sirens.
What was I to do? I felt trapped,
Locked and trapped, too scared to go outside.

I knew I had to do it, so I opened the door to hear people
screaming 'Evacuate!'
I didn't know what to think, leave my house and belongings?
I soon found out what was going on, I felt such hate
Towards the people doing this to our country. Just why?

I gathered my most important belongings
And packed them quickly in a large bag ready to go.
Now I was to leave not knowing where I'd end up,
I'd just see what life brings.
I'm off now, goodbye. Maybe we'll meet again some day.

Gemma Vincent (15)
Sholing Girls' School

ALL ABOUT MATTY

My brother's name is Matty,
He's a bit batty,
But very caring,
And sometimes daring.

He helps me when I'm sad,
Even when I'm bad.
He gets me out of things
But I hate it when he sings.

Sometimes we fight
But he's always right!
He's so cool,
But a bit of a fool!

He's really good at art,
And he's got a heart.
He cheers me up when I'm low,
He's the very best bro!

Rebecca Millington (12)
Sholing Girls' School

THE GRIFFIN

I looked out of the window to see her flutter,
Into the grimy moss filled gutter.
Her feathers were greasy and all smoothed out,
I was so horrified I wanted to shout.
Then she lay still though she was dead,
If I wasn't frozen stiff I would have fled.
Then I gasped with all my might and went to
See if she was alright.
When I got to the moss filled gutter
I heard her evil high voice mutter,
'Crack, crack crackly, crack, crack, crack.'
I picked her up and she felt really light,
Then she took off into flight.
Then I realised and felt like an old hag,
That she wasn't a griffin but a plastic bag!

Laura Paine (12)
Sholing Girls' School

A DREAM

I used to think that I was alone,
But I saw something that changed my tone,
A girl sitting, weeping,
I knew then that I had a family,
A family that cared,
A family that shared.
I felt sorry for the girl
Sitting all alone,
Decided to talk to her.
I crossed the road,
She saw me coming and started to run,
As though I blocked out her sun.
I followed her for a while,
Then I saw her and smiled,
She came towards me,
I put out my hand,
She took it.
We walked away,
Away from the past,
For the future we have a dream,
A dream where everyone has a loving family.
A loving family
And caring friends.

Amy Stapleton (12)
Sholing Girls' School

FEELINGS

Hate is red and black,
and tastes of gone-off pears,
and smells of smelly cheese,
looks like broken glass,
sounds like heavy metal,
feels like you have been stabbed in the back.

Love is baby pink and baby blue,
tastes like sweet strawberries,
smells like fresh roses, just been grown,
looks like a sunset in the sky,
sounds like singing birds in the trees,
feels like a gentle breeze in your ear.

Samantha Page (12)
Sholing Girls' School

ON CHRISTMAS DAY

It was Christmas, the snow was falling,
Birds singing like a low note on a flute.
I love Christmas,
Snowman building,
Cold snow going through my hands,
And don't forget the yummy roast dinner.

I can't wait to open my presents,
I told my mum I wanted a big, glittering, sparkling red bike,
I can't wait to open the present and see the bike.
First I took off the wrapping paper,
Then I saw a Barbie,

Then another,
Then I came to the last present.
I took off the paper very slowly,
And then I saw the biggest red bike.
I had never seen anything like it before.

'I love it,' I said to my mum and dad.

Kelly King (11)
Sholing Girls' School

LOVE

Love is a flower reaching for the sun,
Love can be laughter, love can be fun.
There's love for your family, there's love for your friends,
There's love and there's hatred but love never ends.

I love my family, my mum and my dad,
Without love this world would go mad.
Miss beating hearts and roses in bloom,
Drinking champagne with the stars and the moon.

There's love for your family, there's love for your friends,
There's love and there's hatred but love never ends.

Gemma May (14)
Sholing Girls' School

JOY AND HAPPINESS

Happiness is bright orange,
it tastes like sweet toffee,
it smells like white roses
in a green, rolling field,
it sounds like people laughing,
happiness is joyful.

Joy is yellow,
it tastes like ice-cream
and smells of daffodils.
Joy looks like a pot of red and blue flowers,
it sounds like cats miaowing,
it feels like a golden sunset.

Naomi Miles (12)
Sholing Girls' School

ONE LOST CAT

There once was a cat on the road one day,
His fur was as black as night.
When I went to pick him up he was as fine as hay,
You could see it, especially when you went through lights.

Oh I brought him home and fed him chopped bacon,
He looked so surprised at the sight,
That when he was eating it, he was rather shaken,
Oh he probably slept like a wink that night.

When my mum saw the cat,
'Oh my goodness,' she said,
'now we can't have that.'
'But I let him have a bed.'
'My dear child, that does not matter.'
'But Mum, he has eyes in his head.'
'Even if you gave him a pound of butter,
                    it still wouldn't matter.'

So that day, I took it back to that road,
He ran off instantly, then he slipped in a gate,
Then he bumped into a toad.
Then he looked at this girl as if to say, 'Sorry I'm late.'
The girl saw that I looked at her with a sad eye,
So she said that I could have one of his kittens.
My eyes then twinkled like a cherry on a pie,
And I lived happily ever after with my kitten
                    named Mitten.

Sarah Wiltshire (12)
Sholing Girls' School

GRAVE OF REGRET

Sweet angel come to me,
Show me your true identity,
Come now upon thy heavenly grave,
Sing sweet songs, strong and brave.

A tear drips down my mother's face,
I wish she could just see my grace,
My windswept memories thrown away,
I always forgot just to say

Unspoken words, too late to say.
I watched her walk around the bay,
I left her standing all alone,
If I had just picked up the phone,

To say, 'I'm sorry for what I've done.'
Maybe then we could have some fun,
Some time together,
For ever and ever.

'Oh Mother, please forget that day,
That you and I had little to say,'
I walked off, I walked away.
Why did I not stay?

I thought I had done my best
The truth was, I'd set the test.
This test we played,
We let it fade.

If I had replaced those words of shame
With lovely words, not the game
Of love and war - forgive me please,
We should both feel at ease.

I wish I was,
I *wish* I was
With her today,
Just to say,
'Mother, I love you and always will.'

Larissa Pearce (13)
Sholing Girls' School

MYSERY

I like a good poem,
full of strange creatures.
Tension, suspense,
And all of the features.

Goblins and ghosts
making weird sounds,
mysterious footsteps
walking upon the ground.

From the sound of the wind,
to the rattling of chains,
seeing poltergeists,
playing card games.

Tales have been told,
stories have been said.
Beware when you read them
As you might wake the dead!

Laura Peeke (15)
Sholing Girls' School

HAPPINESS

Happiness is bright orange and yellow,
it tastes like fresh, ripe, strawberries,
it smells like fresh spring flowers,
it looks like a warm lake rippling along,
it sounds like children laughing in the sun,
it feels like warm grass in the sunset.

Joy is bright yellow and green,
it tastes like roast chicken on a plate,
it smells like rice pudding,
it looks like a rose that has just been picked,
it sounds like hymns,
it feels like a warm, bubbly bath.

Anger is dark grey and black,
it tastes like snails,
it smells like bubbling boils,
it looks like a dead man's head with an axe,
it sounds like a chill,
it feels like a shiver up your back.

Katrina Waddington (12)
Sholing Girls' School

LOVE IS IN THE AIR

Love, it is bright pink,
It tastes like bread pudding,
It smells like apples and pies,
It looks like candles in the dark,
It sounds like birds singing in the dark.
Sound is love in the air,
It is romantic.

Blue is the shore,
It tastes like seaweed,
It smells like the air,
It looks beautiful,
It sounds like waves moving,
The shore is blowing and waving.

Hayley Jacobs (12)
Sholing Girls' School

I WENT TO THE ZOO

My name is Sara and
I have a great mother and father.

They took me to the zoo to see the kangaroos.
They kicked and punched
And did everything that kangaroos do.

They also took my brother Perry,
And he decided to take his
Boxing gloves and have a go too.

They also took me on a picnic
And that was good too.

There was also a giraffe,
He really made me laugh.

And a monkey that was funky
And he was cheeky and funny.

We sat in the park
Until it got dark,
To join the animals too!

Sara Webb (11)
Sholing Girls' School

MAGIC!

What is magic?
Is it tricks?
Is it ghosts?
Is it vampires?
Is it alive?
It must be something,
it is very mysterious,
does it ever end?
Is it a never-ending circle?
Is it just plain magic?
Magic.
No, it's not tricks,
No it's not ghosts,
No, it's not vampires,
No, it's not alive,
Yes, it is something!
Yes, it is mysterious,
Yes, it does end.
No, it's not a never-ending circle
And
Yes, it is just plain magic!

Esther Collier
Sholing Girls' School

HATE

Hate is black,
It tastes like burnt toast with marmalade,
Smells like cheesy feet,
Looks like mud pie,
Sounds like breaking glass,
Feels like an argument and you
Don't want to make up with your mates.

Anger is purple,
Tastes like purple pudding,
Smells like mouldy cheese,
Looks like a red ball rolling down the road,
Sounds like arguing going on,
Feels like a baby crying.

Kimberley Hawkins (12)
Sholing Girls' School

ALL HALLOW'S EVE IN THE DEPTHS OF ATLANTIS

It's that time of year
It's come again to weep upon our souls.
A hidden secret of a lost world.
Beneath the cruel waves
How hidden can a world be
To not be found for an eternity?
All Hallow's Eve, a celebration
Under death-ridden waves.
Eternity is not forever.
But forever and a day.
You hear the cries of lost souls
From that terrible evening.
Not this year will people
Stand in graveyards.
They will know the truth.
No longer waiting in silence
Trapped in a watery world.
People trapped against their will.
Dead to the world as if not exciting.
They will be let free to the night.
On All Hallow's Eve
They fight to the surface once more.

Jess Thompson (13)
Sholing Girls' School

DAYS OF THE WEEK

A Monday morning,
I rise from my bed,
My tired eyes awake.

A terrible Tuesday,
I wake up feeling grey,
My eyes fall on the grey sky.

A wonderful Wednesday,
I open my eyes to the sight of the sun,
I feel great.

A tearful Thursday,
My eyes fill with water,
I feel upset.

A fearful Friday,
I sit and watch the frightening skies,
Thunder disturbs me.

A sleepy Saturday,
My eyes close,
I fall asleep.

A sunny Sunday,
Sun blinds me,
Smell of roast dinner wafts by.

Hayley Lovett (11)
Sholing Girls' School

AUTMN

Trees shivering in the cold north wind,
throwing the dancing leaves to the ground
to make a crunchy blanket of gold and red, yellow and brown,
leaving the trees undressed and cold.

The clocks go back for a dark night,
ready for a Hallowe'en fright.
Spooky lanterns made out of pumpkins
with scary faces glowing in the night,
Children laugh, shouts of joy, all shouting in a loud voice,
'Trick or treat or something to eat!'

Katie Cobb (12)
Sholing Girls' School

FUTURE

Future's bright,
There will be no more fights,
No hunger, no homeless.

No racists, no stealing,
No criminals, no hate,
No sadness, no abortions either,
No fostering, or adoptions needed,
No deserted people, no diseases.

The future's bright
Because there will be peace,
Yes to happiness and love.

Cures for all diseases,
Food for everyone in the world,
With equal opportunities.

To be where you want to be,
To be who you want to be,
Whatever you want to be.

Nicola Bricknell (12)
Sholing Girls' School

MILLENNIUM POEM

The millennium is only about two months away,
it is coming faster and faster every day.
Everybody believes there will be a Millennium Bug,
it might just happen, so don't push it under the rug!
I can't wait to know what the future will hold,
Whatever happens, I think everyone should be told.

Lots of people will celebrate the two thousandth year,
when Big Ben strikes twelve there will be a loud cheer.
On New Year's Day people will visit the Millennium Dome,
There will be lots to see and do, they will even forget about
                                            going home.

The year two thousand only comes once in a lifetime,
Now that it's here, we realise it's been a long climb.

Katie Egan (12)
Sholing Girls' School

BRUSHING YOUR TEETH

Brush your teeth
Twice a day
And tooth decay
Will stay away.
In the morning,
In the evening,
Even when you have
Finished eating.
Colgate, Macleans, Total Fresh,
So what?
They all do their very best.

Kayleigh Tench (13)
Sholing Girls' School

THE YOUNG GIRL

The young girl was flung into a cell,
Her thoughts, 'What's to happen to me now?'
Charged with murder the day before,
Nothing could go wrong anymore,

She heard the door slam behind her
And hoped that someone would come in and find her,
Before her execution the next day,
When she would go to heaven and fly away.

The light went off,
The room went silent,
She sat down and coughed
And then she turned violent.

She stood up and threw a chair
Right across the room,
Apart from the chair, the room was bare,
And it was filled with gloom.

The bell rung the next day,
Where she found out she would have to pay
For doing the dreadful thing she did
And killing a four year-old called Sid.

As she walked out into the cold and damp,
She realised she felt just like a tramp,
And what would happen to her now,
Will it hurt or sting, would she say 'Ow!'?

Everyone was shouting and screaming,
The person got down off the stage where she was cleaning,
Will she go to heaven or hell?
She doesn't know, but she's going now.

Louise Spreadbury (13)
Sholing Girls' School

THE HAUNTED HOTEL

The house was standing dark,
No one dare to go there,
They say there's spirits in the hotel,
I think they're just dreaming.

When the clock strikes twelve,
They say they see a ghost,
It seems very strange to me,
It must be some sort of hoax.

I stayed there for a night,
Oh boy, did I get a fright.
There was a man walking down the corridor,
I didn't stop to see.

I went screaming in the street,
Don't dare go in that house,
Or even stay the night.
I tell you something, you'll be out
As fast as you went in.

Carlie Tejada (13)
Sholing Girls' School

FUN THINGS

Happiness is yellow,
it tastes like grapes,
it smells like bananas,
it looks like a bright summer's day,
it sounds like a gentle cat's purr,
it feels like a golden sunset.

Love is pink,
it tastes like apples, it smells like roses,
it looks like my mum,
it feels like a new baby girl.

Joy is light blue,
it tastes like pineapple,
it smells like pears,
it looks like peaches,
it feels like my hamster.

Emma Munro (13)
Sholing Girls' School

MY LITTLE HAMSTER

I pamper my hamster,
It's fine and well.
It needs lots of treats,
Especially Shredded Wheat.

My hamster sleeps
In a heap
And leaps around my feet.
When I'm in bed,
She sleeps by my head.

She's brown and white
And very bright,
She wakes in the night,
Because she doesn't like light.

She climbs and scratches
And chews the bars,
But I love her to bits,
She's my number one hit.

Sarah Johnston (11)
Sholing Girls' School

LITTLE FOXES

Little foxes playing around,
Making lots and lots of sound.
Their mother calls, 'Time for bed,
Come and rest your sleepy heads.'

The little foxes carry on playing,
Unaware of what Mum's saying,
They're too busy having fun
In the scorching midday sun.

Mother shouts, 'Come on you lot,
There's rabbit stew here in the pot,
If you don't come right away,
Dad and I will eat the lot!'

The foxes decide it's time to run,
The race is on, oh what fun!
Home to eat the yummy dinner,
I wonder who will be the winner?

Claire Doherty (12)
Sholing Girls' School

I HAVE A DREAM

I have a dream that I could ride a horse for 100 miles,
Gallop and canter is all I'd do,
So that I could get off from having lessons.
Jump and laugh, never fall off, that's what I want to be able to do.
Go to shows and at least come third,
But I guess that will all be in my dreams.
But for now I shall be happy in the school,
Learning how to sit and trot as well as I can do.

Jade Gibson (13)
Sholing Girls' School

ANIMALS

I love cats and dogs and mice,
I think that they are really nice,
I like to hold them in my arms,
They help me think and make me calm.

Bunnies, hamsters, gerbils, rats,
These are the ones that are chased by cats,
They scurry about in corners and cracks,
Trying to find tasty snacks.

Sometimes animals cause laughter,
But they also need to be looked after,
Especially when there's terrible weather,
They bring the whole family together.

Gillian Jackson (13)
Sholing Girls' School

BULLY

The bully is a devil,
he rises up from the dead,
and when you're naughty,
he'll smack you round the head.

As he is by the corner shop
eating his sweets,
he meets another boy,
also eating sweets.

They talk,
they walk away,
they stop, and meet another day,
the bully stops to play.

Sophie Olive (11)
Sholing Girls' School

FOOTBALL CRAZY!

Football is a funny game,
Eleven men a side,
The goal at which to aim the ball
Seems rather large and wide.

Different colours for each team
On the field you'll see,
Green is for the goalie,
And black for the referee.

Football is a nation's game
Played all around the world,
Many fans will want to see
Their winning flag unfurled.

The Dell is home to our boys,
'Come on you Saints!' we shout.
Southampton is our premier team,
Now that should have some clout.

Nicola Regular (12)
Sholing Girls' School

HALLOWE'EN

Black cat,
Scary bat,
Frightening witch,
See-through ghost,
Red devil,
Spooky skeleton,
Green man,
Bright orange pumpkins.

Carla Rickards (11)
Sholing Girls' School

FAIRY RHYME

Once long ago
In a land called Bubbalo
Was a little house,
Which had a little mouse.
There in the house lived the wolf and his gran,
And a lot of junk like pots and pans.
One fine day
In the middle of May,
The wolf went on his walk
And on his way had a talk to some pigs just moving in.
Their names were Zap, Zen and Zin.
The pigs were building an apartment
Which was really not the wolf's department.
The wolf had just reached the berry bush,
When the wind started to violently *whoosh*.
He quickly started to turn back home,
Knowing that he should have brought his lucky stone.
On passing the pigs again, they invited him in for supper,
And if he was good, maybe a cuppa!
The third pig then came along with the gran, dead, for dinner,
The pig had even gone and skinned her.
The wolf not knowing it was his grandma, ate her up
Without a but,
Then the pigs declared once more that they were starving,
Then the knives started carving.
The wolf was devoured in a second,
Or so a passer by reckoned.
Now there is no more to be said,
As both the grandma and the wolf are dead.

Andrea Houghton (12)
Sholing Girls' School

KIAN POEM

Kian is so lovely and sweet, I wish he was chocolate,
he's good enough to eat!
I wish I could bite into him and chew on him all day,
He wouldn't taste like normal chocolate,
He would taste yummy in his own special way.
I want to kiss his lips that taste like a Mars bar,
Then he can buy me a very expensive car.
It should be made out of Crunchie,
Which is so lovely and nice,
Or maybe the creamy Angel Delight.
I have such a difficult time to decide,
I find it so hard to make up my mind.
Kian, chocolate, Crunchie, Delight,
I have to stay up all night.
All I want people to know
Is that I love Kian so.

Kate McArthur (13)
Sholing Girls' School

FIRST DAY AT SCHOOL

I went to my new school,
I saw the headteacher, she was mean,
And she did look a little green.
It was scary and I hoped no one was hairy,
there were loads of teachers about shouting everywhere,
And pulling out their hair.
'Come over here my dear, is this your first day?
I was wondering, would you like to go out to play?'
'Yes I would like to go out to play,
And thank you for my wonderful day.'

Samantha Bowers (11)
Sholing Girls' School

FLOWERS

Some flowers have big petals,
Some petals are small,
The stems are green
And some stems grow tall.

There are roses, tulips
Buttercups and daisies,
Sunflowers, bluebells,
My favourites are pansies.

We pick flowers
To make us feel better,
We send them to people
With a little letter.

There are flowers everywhere,
Even on my lawn.
I planted some yesterday,
Soon a baby bud will be born.

Stacey Gardner (13)
Sholing Girls' School

THE CHRISTMAS NIGHT

I've been waiting all night for Christmas to arrive,
It's here, it's on its way, I'm glad I'm still alive.
Now it's time to open my eyes,
I hope it's a surprise.
I run downstairs to open my present from Dad.
It has flowers and roses on it, it was a writing pad.
My other present was from Mum, it was a fluffy jumper,
With a picture of Thumper.

Natalie Crow (11)
Sholing Girls' School

AUTUMN LEAVES

Leaves falling everywhere,
Flying through the frosty air.
Whisking about in the sky,
All the colours dark and light.
Brown, yellow and green,
With such a golden sheen.
All shapes and sizes,
As precious as prizes.
Some are crumpled, some are straight,
Some are old and out of date.
They fall to the ground
Not making a sound.
As they fall they tend to swirl,
As they fly so swiftly by,
I often wonder why.
Why they fall straight to the ground,
And don't stay high safe and sound.
But after all they have to go,
So other leaves have time to grow.

Michelle Brazier (13)
Sholing Girls' School

UNTITLED

The boy next door
was only four,
he always played
on the floor.

His name was Roy,
he had lots of toys,
he was very coy
because he was a boy.

The girl next door was more,
she was ten and four.
The boy hit the girl and she was very sore,
that's because her behaviour was very poor.

Rebekah Spranklin (11)
Sholing Girls' School

PIGS

Pigs are special,
Pigs are nice.
Pigs go well
With egg fried rice!

Pigs are friendly,
Pigs are great.
Pigs put pork chops
On your plate!

Pigs are barmy,
Pigs are nutty.
Pigs provide
A nice bacon butty!

Pigs get jealous,
Pigs can boast.
Pigs taste great
In a Sunday roast!

Pigs are greedy,
Pigs tell lies.
Pigs are made
Into little pork pies!

Samantha Harmer (12)
Sholing Girls' School

MY FAMILY

My sister is like a shadow,
always following me around.
My sister can be very sweet,
although she isn't very neat.

My mum is kind and generous,
always letting me go out,
she only says no
if I really start to pout.

My dad is very serious,
he never gets delirious,
he sometimes argues with my mum
and then I start to suck my thumb.

Chantelle Harrison (12)
Sholing Girls' School

HALLOWE'EN

H   allowe'en is fun,
A   lso scary,
L   ittle kids go to bed early,
L   oving every minute of it,
O   ut of the house the children go,
W   aving to their parents as they say goodbye,
E   veryone's screaming and running about,
E   ven the parents are having fun,
N   ightmares occurring.

Jamila Gibson (12)
Sholing Girls' School

THE FANTASTIC WITCH

There was an old witch,
All she did was stitch.
She looked after cattle
And ended up in a battle.

She wore a brace
Which came halfway down her face,
She had a black cat
That wore a hat.

She saw a child
Who was very wild,
She got in her car
But not to go far.

She went to the shops
And started to hop,
She said 'Hi' to a pie
Instead of the sky.

When she got home,
She saw a bone,
She felt very sick
And then did a trick.

She went to bed,
But bumped her head,
She saw some stars
Then landed on Mars.

She couldn't get back
To see her cat,
So she just sat
And that was that.

Tia Scott (12)
Sholing Girls' School

MY MUM

My mum is the best thing in the world,
Although she shouts at me
I'll never stop caring or loving her,
Although she can be mean.

I will love Mum forever more,
Because she is my life.
The only way we'll be broken up
Is if I lose my life.

If something comes between us
Which I know will never come,
Because I love my mum so much,
I wouldn't be that dumb.

My mum is the best thing in the world,
Although she shouts at me,
I will never stop caring or loving her,
Because we are a team.

Abbey Granger (12)
Sholing Girls' School

ROSY, MY BIRD

All the colours of the rainbow and playful as well,
Looking in the mirror then bashing her bell,
Having a bath, oh what fun as she splashes water on herself.
Rosy is my parrot, taking titbits from my hand,
She is a good friend to me and makes me feel so grand.

Laura Jones (11)
Sholing Girls' School

MY PERFECT MEN!

A lovely man is James William Van Der Beek,
I like the way he always speaks,
If I could meet him
I'd likely be shy,
Though I wouldn't let the moment pass me by.
We'd go out together for a meal,
From that moment on, the day would be special.

Another man who always catches my eye,
Is David Boreanaz, he's a really sweet guy.
I would love to meet him and go on a date,
I would arrive early
To not make him wait.
As soon as our eyes meet,
The earth will shake and quake,
And we'll spend our lives together,
Like on an endless date.

Samantha Scott (13)
Sholing Girls' School

MONDAY

It is Monday,
The day of school,
Come on,
It's time to go to school,
But . . . but . . . but . . .
I feel ill Mum.
Come on, come on, miss,
You cannot miss school,
It is Monday!

Stephanie Orr (11)
Sholing Girls' School

BUMBLE

Bumble is a little dog,
A dog that's full of joy,
A dog that likes to play with toys
And sleep throughout the day.

Bumble is a star dog,
On water or on land,
But when on Baby Bellis studying the log,
By the helm she would stand.

Bumble is a travelling dog
In the Discovery she would sleep,
When her master's car would stop,
Out she wants to leap.

Bumble is no trouble
When at October Cottage she plays,
Waiting for the 25th,
To party on her master's 60th.

Kathryn Churchill (12)
Sholing Girls' School

MY PET RABBIT

My fluffy rabbit is a good friend,
But bites me in the throat,
The best pet you can get,
She will make a good fur coat.

Laura Chandler (11)
Sholing Girls' School

ALL ABOUT SADIE

There was an old lady,
Her name was Sadie,
She lived in a cottage,
When it was at its hottest.

She went to the shop
With her shoes in a knot,
She tripped up and banged her head,
Then went home to bed.

The next day
She took her grandchildren to play,
They went to the park
And stayed out till dark.

Their Mum went mad
And phoned their Dad,
They came back at nine,
Because they couldn't tell the time.

They shouted at her
And took the children to the car,
They drove home,
Then picked up the phone.

It was all moan, moan,
Then they slammed down the phone.
The next day,
Their Mum came round to say,

'I'm sorry,
You got stuck behind a lorry
And got home at nine,
But you should learn how to tell the time.'

Emma Moncrieff (12)
Sholing Girls' School

TEACHERS?

Teachers are the worst thing in life
because they shout at you when you are having fun.
Every one of them thinks they can go and relax
during the lunchtime in the sun.
All teachers think they are great
'Cause they know everything,
Classrooms have to be spotless they say,
But it's their desks which are the dirtiest.
Having a teacher can sometimes be great,
But sometimes they holler and shout,
Rather them than me!
So what are your teachers like?
Just the same as mine?
Smelly and nasty?
So what are they like?

Sarah Critchley (12)
Sholing Girls' School

MY DOG

My dog is a Labrador,
He likes going to explore,
My dog is the colour yellow,
He is such a good little fellow.
He likes to play ball,
He can jump over a wall,
He likes to dream, but he loves ice-cream.
His favourite ice-cream is chocolate now,
I have taught him how to bow,
He will be my friend,
Right until the very end.

Joanne Cox (13)
Sholing Girls' School

MY FAMILY

I love my family, they are the best,
They are enjoyable and always beat the rest.

My dad thinks he owns the moon,
He runs after me with the wooden spoon.

My mum, she is great,
But never lets me on a date.

I hate my brother and he hates me,
But when we're in a good mood, we make peace be.

My sister is the annoying one,
But sometimes we have lots of fun.

My family are the best
And will always beat the rest.

Amy Clune (12)
Sholing Girls' School

STAR

Star, star up in the sky,
Twinkle light, twinkle bright,
Twinkle all through the night.
Twinkle for you, twinkle for me,
Twinkle for all the happiness around me,
Star, star up in the sky.

Claire Callaway (12)
Sholing Girls' School

NIGHT!

Stars shining bright
Through the night
In the sky above.

Then comes the sun,
It's only just begun,
The light streaks through the curtains.

It's scary, it's creepy, it's night, night, night,
Monsters appear, they're alive they're alive,
Help me! Then a light appears.

The monsters are dead and all bad things are in bed,
The light is good and I'm not scared,
For nothing can hurt me.

Hooray, hooray, it's day, day, day, then I wake up,
I'm in a sweat,
I see my mum and smile . . .
            I remember the terrible things I dreamt.

Hannah Scully (12)
Sholing Girls' School

MY DOG BENJ

My dog Benji is a Staffordshire bull terrier,
Always bouncing and jumping around.
I'm surprised he doesn't bump his head on the ground.
Warming hugs and kisses when you get home.
Personally, my dog is very cool.
He likes his ball,
But mostly food and drink overall.

Kelly West (12)
Sholing Girls' School

MY GRANDMOTHER

All day long she just sits there
In her wooden rocking chair,
She has no feelings, she has no thoughts,
All she does is what she's taught,
She sits there staring into space,
She doesn't realise she's in the human race,
She used to be head of the Navy,
That was when her hair was wavy,
She used to be a lively old thing,
Always jolly, wanting to sing,
But now she always is asleep,
Always in a dreamworld very deep,
But no matter whatever they say,
She always knows how to make my day.

Rebecca Browne (12)
Sholing Girls' School

IT SHOULDN'T MATTER

Some people have
Yellow, brown, black or white skin,
But it doesn't matter.
Some people speak
English, Scottish, German or French,
but it doesn't matter.
Some people have
Pink, red, purple or ginger hair.
There skin, language and hair
Should not matter.

Natasha Head (12)
Sholing Girls' School

CLASS TIME THOUGHTS

Class by class,
It goes on all day,
I wonder if it will stop
So we can play.

Stuck in here
for many years,
If we do not escape,
I'm sure there'll be tears.

Different teachers,
Young and old,
All have one problem,
To make you do as you're told.

My friends are here,
And they all care.
I have no fear
When they are there.

The teachers are nice,
But some get mad
When the class gets rowdy
And behaves very bad.

Heidi Ross (12)
Sholing Girls' School

THE MOON

The moon is gold,
The moon is bright,
It always shines with all its might.

There's a man in the moon
As you can see,
Always smiling down at me.

The moon lights the sky at night,
Covering up the gloomy sight.

But when the sun rises in the morning,
The tired and sleepy moon is yawning.

Lucy Ellison (12)
Sholing Girls' School

TONIGHT IS THE NIGHT!

Coffins creak open
The zombies jump out
The tombstones shatter
Everyone runs and shouts
Hallowe'en is upon us
It's that time of year
When all humans scream
And all zombies cheer.

The brew is bubbling
The spell is cast
The witches are ready
You had better run fast.

The werewolves are howling
And ready to kill
Their teeth are so sharp
It gives you a chill.

The ghosts wake from slumber
They fly into the night
They are joined by all demons
To give you a fright!

Kelly Parker (13)
Sholing Girls' School

MY FAMILY AND MY FRIENDS

My mum is always in a fuss,
My friend called Amy catches the bus.

My dad thinks he is always the boss,
He goes down to the pub and spends his dosh.

My sister moans all day long,
When she moans I sing a song.

My brother is like a hairy mole,
He I so skinny like a pole.

My friend called Abbey dyed her hair,
And now it's gone kind of fair.

My friend called Amy likes to talk,
We both took my dog for a walk.

Laura Finch (12)
Sholing Girls' School

AUTUMN FIREWORKS

Fireworks come at autumn,
When the leaves are falling down,
Swirling, twirling, falling down to the ground.
But at night when all is dark and quiet,
Suddenly an abundance of colour, and sound.
Catherine wheels and rockets,
Big bangs and loud crashes,
All animals fear for the fifth of November.
The banging and crashing with a splash of colour comes,
But after this it is quiet.

Winter slowly comes,
Carefully a creeping in,
As my fingers and toes are feeling numb.
Oh, how I long for the swirling and twirlingness,
And colour of autumn.

Katie Walker (12)
Sholing Girls' School

CATS

Cats are sleek, cats are slim
They sleep all day and act all dim
What they do at night, nobody knows
I wonder if they've made any foes.
They have velvet-soft fur and big, sharp claws
They come from tigers but do not roar.
They scratch up the carpet and look very pretty
Then go back to being a soft kitty.
They're all different colours and all different patterns
They concentrate their eyes on the fire in the lantern.
They curl up on my lap and keep me warm
They go into shape and keep their form.
Cats have whiskers to judge their distances
They always hop through different clearances
They have a gentle and graceful purr
Along with their velvet-soft fur.
Cats are sleek, cats are slim
They sleep all day and act all dim.

Stacey Drew (13)
Sholing Girls' School

MILLENNIUM

Hooray it's 2000, everyone screams and shouts,
Champagne drinking, people thinking
what's it all about?
2000 years, everybody cheers but what's good about that?
Millennium Babies, everyone's crazy at £100,000 for
the bunch.
One century ago people wouldn't know that computers were
all the rage.
But then comes this Bug, it's not nice to hug,
It eats all the computers up.
The world would be stuck with such little luck
but this is the turn of the century.
But all's said and done, so let's have some fun
and celebrate millennium 2000.

Fern Abraham (12)
Sholing Girls' School

THE DOWN AND OUT

Nobody likes me
I am all alone
In the big, wide world.
No friends,
No family,
No one cares,
No one thinks about me,
I am alone in the big, wide world.
No fun to share,
No one to love,
I am crying here and there.
I live alone on the streets,
As the dark, rainy nights go on.

Joanne Hallett (12)
Sholing Girls' School

LOVE DREAM

You love him,
He loves you,
You like pink,
He likes blue.
You like his eyes,
The greeny blue,
He likes your hair,
Fresh and new.
The way you sway,
The way you walk,
The way he grins,
The way he talks.
The sweat on your
Forehead glistens
And gleams,
Then you wake up,
It was just a dream!

Sophie Barnes (13)
Sholing Girls' School

CHRISTMASTIME

Christmas is on its way,
Not long to go.
Christmas trees will be up soon,
Everybody jumping around, getting excited.

Looking forward to all those presents,
Being home with my
Friends and family,
All getting together.

Enjoy Christmas.

Amy Gordon (12)
Sholing Girls' School

CARTOONS

Cartoons are funny things,
You use your imagination
With lots of smiles and big noses.
You can do anything with a cartoon,
You can make them sad or grumpy,
Happy or surprising.
You can do anything with a cartoon,
You can dress them up in big bow ties
Or really baggy trousers.
You can do anything with a cartoon,
You can give them big, floppy ears
Like Bugs Bunny,
Or make them spin and shout just like Taz.
You can do anything with a *cartoon!*

Rachel Masterman (12)
Sholing Girls' School

HALLOWE'EN

Ghouls and ghosts,
black cats and full moons,
bats' wings and 'trick or treating',
apple bobbing, scary pumpkins,
devils and vampire blood.
These are the things that make Hallowe'en special,
fancy dress parties and lots of sweets,
throwing eggs and knocking on doors.
Ghouls and ghosts,
black cats and full moons,
bats' wings and 'trick or treating',
apple bobbing, scary pumpkins,
devils and vampire blood.

Rebecca Churcher (12)
Sholing Girls' School

COLOURS OF EVERYDAY LIFE!

Green is for jealousy, envy and greed.
Blue is for sadness and moods.
Red is for anger and white for calm.
Pink is for babies, cuddles galore.
Peach is the colour of young girls' cheeks.
Yellow is for those who run away.
Orange, lemon and lime, the colours of citrus fruits.
Turquoise, for the colour of the deep, deep sea.
Gold, for the sand on the beaches.
Silver, for the moon and stars.
Black for the night that surrounds them.
Purple, for the colour of the wrapping on a Dairy Milk.
Brown is the dirt which wonderful flowers grow of many colours.
Without the sun the colours would not grow.
Without the colours the days would be dreary and dull.

Julianne Ediss (13)
Sholing Girls' School

MY FRIEND, CLAIRE

Claire, Claire has very long hair,
Her eyes are blue and her hair is fair.
She's a good friend to you and me,
And is often round for tea.
She has rosy-red lips,
And long fingertips.
She comes from Surrey,
And she's allergic to curry.
She's always wearing something new,
So come and be her friend too.

Emma Othen (13)
Sholing Girls' School

GORILLAS

My gorilla's called Godzilla,
he's very big and hairy.
He likes eating bananas,
and can get very scary.

He stamps around the jungle,
for nearly all the day.
Apart from when he's eating,
and then he goes away.

If you annoy him, then he'll get mad,
when he's mad you wouldn't like him.
He can get very vicious,
and sometimes even dim.

So that's my gorilla,
his name's Godzilla.
He's big and hairy,
and a bit of a killer.

Michelle Moore (12)
Sholing Girls' School

CATS

Cats are lazy, they sleep all day,
They go out at night and like to play,
They prowl the streets to catch their prey,
But never lose their way.
In the morning, they're waiting to be fed,
Then they wander off to bed.

Kirsty Forder (12)
Sholing Girls' School

UP TO YOUR BEDROOM!

My mum always told me never to lie,
'Coz if she found out, I would cry.
Then she'd get angry, shout and say:
'Up to your bedroom for the rest of the day!'

'It really wasn't my fault, Mum it isn't fair,
I trod on her bag accidentally but then she pulled my hair!'
And as before she began to shout and say,
'Up to your bedroom for the rest of the day!'

In the end I just gave in,
I'd really had enough,
All the blame was put on me,
Parents' rules sure are *tough!*

Katie Large (12)
Sholing Girls' School

RAINFOREST

R ainforests
A re always in colour
I   n every corner of the forest
N ice looking plants and animals
F   lowers are always blooming
O range sun, gleaming
R ain falling down upon the
E arthy floor
S treams run by and soak into the ground
T o help the trees grow and grow.

Clare Guy (13)
Sholing Girls' School

HOMELESS, COLD AND EMPTY

Homeless she sat by the boarded up window,
Hand still outstretched for the food that she needs,
Inside her, not only her stomach is starving
But her heart is pleading for love.

Her mother has put her there, too poor to keep her,
Hoping that someone will recognise need,
But no one is kindly to small, dirty children,
And so she is left there,
Her heart to bleed.

As they look at her old clothes and grubby face,
What a horrible wretch they say,
She watches with empty and sorrowful eyes,
They turn up their noses as they walk away.

Bethan Lye (13)
Sholing Girls' School

DOLPHINS

Dolphins are special,
Not any old mammal,
They can be supernatural,
Or your very best friend,
And will be with you till the very end.

Dolphins are supernatural,
They talk to you all,
They really are the nicest animal,
And they will never drive you round the bend,
They are the nicest present you could send.

Leanne Tuck (12)
Sholing Girls' School

UNSETTLED LOVE

I have never felt such love before,
to hold you close and love you more,
Dreamy eyes and padlocked lips,
So tender and desired to kiss.
Lie down and watch the clouds go by,
and pray that we shall never die.
Our new love does blossom sweet,
You start to feel the morning heat,
Midday arrives, right here and now,
You wipe the sweat from off your brow.
I see the flames dance in your eyes,
So now your evil side shall rise,
Then from my precious heart you tore,
My love for you forever more.

Lauren Jennings (13)
Sholing Girls' School

EARTH, LOVE AND GOD

God made the world,
God made us,
But most of all God made love.

Love is a feeling,
Love is light,
It's not a thing you learn overnight.

Earth is a mystery,
Earth is a zoo
Because it holds everything, even you!

Hollie Whitfield (12)
Sholing Girls' School

THE USUAL MORNING RUSH

'It's 7.30am, time to get up!'
'Mum I want tea, where's my cup?'
'Get ready, stop watching TV!'
'Why do you always shout at me?'
'Do you want cereal or do you want toast?'
'Do you always have to eat the most?'
'But I'm hungry!'
'Stop whining. You're doing my 'ead in!'
'What did I tell you, put your rubbish in the bin!'
'Oh no, I'm late I've gotta be fast!'
'Bye Mum!'
'Finally peace at last!'

Shelley Masters (12)
Sholing Girls' School

HALLOWE'EN

Deep inside the centre of the earth
Where no light can exist.

A fire with the darkest flames
Burns inside the devil's brain.

Demons dancing around a pool
A pool of darkened waves.

The underworld comes out to play
On this Hallowe'en day.

The dressing up just tries to hide
The demons that are riding by.

Lucy Carter (13)
Sholing Girls' School

BONFIRE NIGHT

Last year on the 5th of November,
as far as I can remember,
The day quickly turned into night,
I sat in my room in the dark,
waiting in silence for a spark.
And suddenly it happened,
it shot up high,
and brightened up the sky.
The colours were so lovely,
The pinks, greens, yellows and reds,
The noises woke people in their beds,
The loud bangs and the glowing fires,
The night was something to remember,
Last year on the 5th of November.

Lucie Cottrell (13)
Sholing Girls' School

AUTUMN

Autumn,
The golden leaves floating down from the trees,
No longer green and moist,
Children playing in the piles of moss,
Wrapped up tight in their hats and coats,
That smell of bonfire that's always around,
That foggy mist which hides your view,
of the squirrel that's collecting nuts,
damp from the autumn dew.
That cold moist feeling that seems to say,
'I'm winter and I'm coming your way!'

Samantha Warren (13)
Sholing Girls' School

Boys' Love

Boys always act smart in front of their mates,
to impress the girls and get their dates,
but when they're alone,
they're as shy as a mouse,
they cuddle up close,
with you in the house,
they will write you a letter tied with a ribbon,
sent with a dove and sign it . . .
            With happiness
                    and
                Love.
                - x -

Emma Dack (13)
Sholing Girls' School

New Year's Eve '99

Everyone will party all night long,
At twelve we'll break into a song,
The millennium's here everyone,
At last the Dome is done,
Everyone's having fun.

So now it's time for the millennium show,
Better get a seat in the front row,
Everyone banish all your fears,
It's the best party of all years.

Melanie Beckett (13)
Sholing Girls' School

SCHOOL

S is for slave or so the teachers seem to think.
C is for customer in the school canteen.
H is for hometime at the end of the day.
O is for orders that we have to follow.
O is for old-fashioned, you haven't seen the uniform.
L is for lessons you like.

Rachel Diaper (12)
Sholing Girls' School

FRIENDS

F riends are always there,
R eally, they do care,
I   should know I've got some now!
E ven though we've had the odd row,
N ever will we break up over a stupid row,
D ealing with friends is always hard,
S sometimes our friendship is like a pack of cards.

Charlotte Arnold (13)
Sholing Girls' School

ALIENS

All alone
Lost in space
Inconspicuous creatures
Everlasting
Never-ending
Severely damaged futures.

Nathalie Viana (13)
Sholing Girls' School

DOLPHINS!

Gracefully through waves
Swimming in and out
Dolphins are endangered
They've got long, pointy snouts.

They are very sensitive
They perform water ballet
They are soft and shiny
They swim from Orlando to Calais

Rachel White (13)
Sholing Girls' School

MY BEST FRIEND

My best friend gives me advice
Every day she's extra nice
At weekends we have a great time
My best friend is special
And I'm glad she is mine.

Louise Harrod (13)
Sholing Girls' School

OUT

I'm on the outside,
He's on the in,
When will my future,
And happiness begin?

I watch him smile,
And laugh and play,
And my heart breaks,
Each and every day.

He knows who I am,
A body in the hall,
Boring and silly,
Too fat, too tall.

But I am more,
Hidden away,
I have passions,
I hurt every day.

I want him to know,
Who I am inside,
But I am too shy,
Forever I'll hide.

Why can't I let him,
See the real me?
If I ever could,
So happy I'd be.

Kit Horsburgh (17)
Taunton's Sixth Form College

KITTEN

Miaow . . .
Lying on the cushion,
Snuggled up on the armchair,
Warm and full with a tummy stuffed with fish
And washed down with milk.

Stretch . . .
Reach for the sky and
Blink those wide eyes
Sparkling with youthfulness,
Playing with the images all around
And capturing the movement of the air.

Leap . . .
For the target of the
Soft, springy rug.
Four feet make an impact,
All present and correct,
Ready to explore this great new place.

Pounce . . .
On the giant who
Moves with such pace
And show your contentment
As the hands smooth your fur
And the fingers reshape your ears.

Paw . . .
At the dancing feet,
With the wiggling toes
As they tease you to catch them
And clamp them in your open mouth
Oh! Such tiny, sharp fangs!

Jodie Laysan (17)
Taunton's Sixth Form College

134

DUSK 'TIL DAWN

Look at the ferocious fire resting on the edge of one's sight,
to look directly, I would not advise,
as there's nothing more precious than your eyes.
It slowly crawls towards the blueness,
There it is, a natural man-proof existence.
It lingers in the blue, alone, peaceful
sharing its beauty, with non-deserved receivers.
By midday the spectacle is of huge adoration,
and has met all expectations and a little bit more.
What majestic hand outdid itself in modelling
an out-of-this-world fireball?
As it hangs there, unassisted, fingerprintless,
time is slowly leaving
everything else slowly behind.
The last few moments are those to savour,
a permanent image to those who experienced it.
it gently descends, timely and concisely,
leaving emptiness.

Jason Ryan (16)
Taunton's Sixth Form College

BUBBLES

Three perfect circles,
Born from the wand,
Float down to our world
And magically bond.

Three empty circles,
From darkness to light,
Outshine their colours,
Oily and bright.

Three dancing circles,
Softly they fall,
A circular world,
From a fragile ball.

Three floating circles,
Drifting away,
Swirling, not stopping,
Engaged in their play.

Three dying circles,
Shimmer and shake,
Mirrors of our world
Until they break.

Francesca Fennell (14)
The Atherley School For Girls

EXAMINATIONS

No talking,
No cheating,
Nothing is allowed,
What shall I write?
Help! My pen's run out.

Sitting still,
Wondering what to do,
Looking out the window,
I chew my pencil
Oh no it's snapped.

I put my hand up and wait,
The teacher comes and sorts me out,
But after that there's no excuse,
I'll have to do my maths.

I realise I made a mistake,
I pick up my rubber
Whoopsies
I had dropped it on the floor
I will do without

Then 'Time up' the teacher said,
I don't know how I'll ever pass that exam.

Katherine Ward (11)
The Atherley School For Girls

THE ESCAPE

As I ran frantically, I took one look back,
The asylum stood there,
Cold, hard, unrelenting, surrounded by darkness;
I had to escape.

In front of me stood the meadow,
An open space spread before me.
I ran to it, desperately;
My last hope.

I ran on and on;
My legs grew weary,
And as I took one final look back,
My nightmares returned.

I fell into a deep slumber,
In my dreams, demons danced before me.
Maniacal laughter screeched in my head . . .

And when I awoke, I was back between
the four walls.

Laura Richmond (11)
The Atherley School For Girls

THE DAY I WENT TRESPASSING

Quietly we did creep
Walking softly on our feet
To collect a ball
On the other side of the wall
Quietly we ran past
Making sure we weren't last
Silently we go
Keeping down low.

Scrambling up and down
Over and under mounds
A bird did twitter
And we did jitter.

Finally we believed
We reached the ball, relieved
We couldn't slack,
We had to get back.

Clare Dinham (13)
The Atherley School For Girls

YOU WERE GONE

You were covering my piece of earth like a guardian angel,
watching me from way above.
You fill the sky; grey but light, cold but warm.

Then you fell as a million raindrops,
a million tears, a million drops of sadness.
Spreading your goodness to everyone and everything you touched.
Yet you were gone as a whole, scattered like a broken mirror,
your reflection shattered forever.

You were gone.
And people and the earth cried for you,
ached for you, empty without you.
Their tears fed the earth, brought life, brought happiness.
Like you once did and still do.
You live on.

Now, as rain falls I'm reminded of you.
As stars shine, I'm reminded of you.
As tears flow, I'm reminded of you.
You live on.

Eleanor Cole (17)
The Atherley School For Girls

SNOWY OWL

As white as snow, it looks at mice,
The owl freezes still, it turns to ice.
He beats his wings and takes to flight,
Catching food in the endless night.

Hovering over fields to find more prey,
The owl flies in the moon's ray.
Each star lights up its eyes,
Which you can see in the moonlit skies.

Flying round his territory, its eaves,
Then suddenly the snowy owl sees.
The dawn is breaking, he flies back home,
Goes to sleep, comes back when he hears the night moan.

Emily Sanderson (11)
The Atherley School For Girls

OUT OF A CAR WINDOW

Trees, fields, rivers and lakes,
So many things, they keep me awake.

Houses, apartments, electricity pylons.
All kinds of objects to keep my eye on.

Ladies talking, kids eating chips.
There isn't even time to have a kip.

Horses, cows, sheep and some pigs.
I'm nowhere near bored and this journey's quite big.

All of a sudden we come to a stop,
There's always next time, we'll have a real bop!

Shelley-Anne George (11)
The Atherley School For Girls

MAN

Man O Man
If I had a pound
For every time you pushed me down
Made my heart fly, cry with fear
My dear, I'd be a rich woman.
If I had a pound
For every time you made me drown in an alley
Kept my free spirit caged, in a blaze of fear
My dear, I'd be a rich woman.
If I had a pound
For every time you laid that frown down on me
Made me feel insecure, like a whore
Woke up in blood, like a war
I'd be a rich woman.
I'd be a rich woman
If I got paid, every time I got laid by your lazy race
Watch my face with fear, my dear.
If I had a pound
For every time you made some profound remark about my breasts
Putting me to the test, against all the best tits
Honey I'd throw fits, 'coz I'd be a rich woman.
If I had a pound
For every time you've made a sound, when I'd walk past
Watch my ass with such splendour, wanting to endeavour me.
Feel free to watch my ass, as I pass you by
My heart will fly knowing I'm not a man,
I'm rich because I'm a woman!

Steph Lefler (16)
The Atherley School For Girls

CONFEDERATE MEMORIAL DAY (1928)

The marching armies of the past
Along the Southern plains
Are sleeping now in quiet rest
Beneath the Southern rains.

The bugle call is now in vain
To rouse them from their bed;
To arms they'll never march again -
They are sleeping with the dead.

No more will Shiloh's plains be stained
With blood our heroes shed,
Nor Chancellorsville resound again
To our noble warriors' tread.

For them no more shall reveille
Sound at the break of dawn,
But may their sleep peaceful be
Till God's great judgement morn.

We bow our heads in solemn prayer
For those who wore the grey,
And clasp again their unseen hands
On their Memorial Day.

Paul Kelly (15)
The Gregg School

THE PET RABBIT

Cute, soft and furry,
Are the things that spring to mind,
When you think of a little rabbit,
And its cotton tail behind.

But as I obviously know,
This is not the truth,
You don't think of a creature,
With a dirty protruding tooth!

The smell that comes from bedding,
Is sickening like a bin,
Even this is not as bad,
As the creatures that lurk within.

Food is yet another thing,
But the rabbit thinks it's nice,
Yet when they spill it on the floor,
It attracts flies and mice.

So if you still want to,
Be very stupid and get,
This dirty, smelly creature,
And keep it as your pet.

I suppose that a rabbit,
Is not really so bad,
After all he's the best pet,
That I have ever had.

James Douglas (14)
The Gregg School

HAWK

It is a silent plane gliding quietly
and peacefully through the air. Swift like the wind,
as reckless as a racing driver with no brakes,
as graceful as a ballet dancer, as precise as
a brain surgeon, as colourful as a
rainbow, awaiting a mid-air attack,
always underestimated, as spectacular
as a hissing snake. The hawk.
Better than
an eagle;
my
type
of
bird.

Jonathan Douglas (12)
The Gregg School

MOONLIGHT

Moonlight seeping
Through the trees,
Whispering to each other,
Telling untold secrets.

Wishing, wishing,
With their leaves,
Dark and silvery
Alone and cold.

Dancing shadows
Dash back and forth,
The trees who keep them
Always, always watching.

Vickie Brook Jackson (16)
The Gregg School

TEDDY HOTEL

'Good morning, Sir!' says Alfred as he opens up the doors,
Whilst Francine cleans the pots and Chef Pierre licks his paws.
Lord and Lady Margate are on their honeymoon,
And Contessa of Obessa is escorted to her room.
But poor old Max, the porter, who hasn't got a clue,
Has lost his way again, but, of course, he's only new!
Penelope and Emma are making castles with the sand,
When little Harry cries because Ann lets go his hand.
Mr Loosely combs the area for anything not right,
And Daphne's bought a new dress for she's courting Reg tonight.
Harriet is sitting and, with a sigh, begins to read;
Commander Teddington looks for ships far out on the sea.
Honey Quaver's music fills the whole room with delight,
And Amanda sits, just gleaming, more entrancing than the night.
Archie asks Bonnie-Lou, boldly for a kiss
And out comes Mr Cheese's camera: 'This moment can't be missed!'
Priscilla's feeling lonely as dancing's not her thing,
When along comes her friend Phoebe to do some more painting.

And all the time the bears just dance and dance and dance,
All but one, old Ted, who's wishing on the stars.
And as the night draws on, the stars begin to hide
And the Teddy Hotel floats away upon the morning tide.

Emma Gatrell (15)
The Gregg School

GREEN

Green, green, green,
Green, green, green,
Green, green, green.
It seems so obscene.
Green, green, green.
Green on the green.
But there's dots of colour
Spaced out in between.
There's butterflies and roses
And poppies and posies.
While foxes flash by
And birds in the sky
Flutter and flutter,
And scutter and scutter.
Oh why, oh why
Is there blue in the sky?
Why are clouds fluffy?
Why do birds fly?
But it all boils down,
It seems so obscene
But everything's green.
So green, green, green, green.

James Waldron (11)
The Gregg School

I REMEMBER

I remember playing my electric guitar
and playing a wrong note.

I remember having breakfast
and eating toast.

I remember Christmas
I got lots of presents.

I remember falling off my bike
and hurting myself.

I remember going to school
in my mum's car.

I remember writing
this remember poem!

William Natt (12)
The Gregg School

HUNTER

Moving slowly through the tall, scented, shimmering grasses,
Creeping furtively,
Every muscle tensed for action
It thinks itself silent,
But its presence,
In some intangible way,
Is known by the prey,
As it sits in the centre of the clearing,
Its fur rippling in the breeze.
The beast feels it has nothing to fear
From the lumbering creature,
That is so slow and careless.
It makes the error.
It moves to the other side of the clearing
As the thing suddenly bursts out of cover,
And runs into the animal's partner.
A fist rises,
Sunlight glints on stone.
The fist falls.
The hunt is over.

Simon Pearcey (15)
The Gregg School

TOWNHILL PARK HOUSE

In the distance, across the sunken gardens,
High hedges stand on guard
Towards the sloping terraces, the stone steps lead
To the splendour of Lord Swaythling's home.

The grand gardens, outlined by dry stone walls,
A bright splash of colour in a geometrical design,
The scent of the lavender bushes,
So calming.
The pergola entwined with wisteria,
its mauve flowers fall towards the ground like lanterns.

This magnificent white house,
the focus of my eye.

Jonathon Simmons (11)
The Gregg School

AUTUMN

Leaf-crisper
Voice-lisper
Sun-glower
Wind-blower
Sky-clearer
Winter-nearer
Throat-wheeze
Brown-leaves
Crisp-air
Weather-fair
Nose-numb
Autumn.

Jessica Ellison (11)
The Gregg School

CARPE DIEM

Lose your inhibitions,
set your spirit free.
Don't let your heart be ruled
or dictated by society.
'Carpe diem', the saying goes:
through free veins passion flows.
When people walk in crowds,
dare to walk against
the preconceptions of morals and sense.
Shake your shackles,
shed your chains;
choose behind a desk
or on African plains
Where zebras graze
and cheetahs stride.
Will you choose a pension
above pride?

Tom Luke (16)
The Gregg School

MY POEM

The wind is howling,
while the birds are singing,
the squirrels are scrounging and scuffling
for food.

The leaves are falling to the floor with
a pitter-patter, pitter-patter.

A slight breeze rustles through
the long green and gold thin grass
with creepy-crawlies hiding in it.

Gemma Stanbrook
The Gregg School

THE OLD MAN!

He puts his fingers in his ear
and fiddles with his hearing aid.

With his white, long, bony fingers,
His skin wrinkly with flaky bits falling off his body.

Then he walks with a big hunchback,
and tries to bend over.

His daughter comes to see him
and he says 'Who are you?'

But then she starts to talk to him,
and all he says is 'What did you say?'

To help him walk he uses a brass handled wooden stick
His false teeth are yellow and sticky.

Sara Bradbury (13)
The Gregg School

WORDS

Words have always been there
Through love, hope and despair
But when you kiss me
My words just fly away
As if they hadn't been there.
My mind is blank,
But my heart is clear.

Anna-Marie Smith (12)
The Mountbatten School

AN EXPLANATION OF WHY INTERIOR DESIGNERS ARE INSANE

Ah, so this is the kitchen is it?
I'm sure we can do lots with this.

You said you wanted cool colours.
Peppermint green paint
Would be perfect on the walls,
If one pasted lilac purple on the ceiling,
And chucked in a good old marble fireplace.

The main feature could be the arch,
With chrome sheets
And flourishes of gleaming gold leaf.
Hang a glitterball from it and see the effect.
Knock down this wall and there'll be room for your own bar.

Arrgh! Remove that vile piece of furniture.
I feel quite faint. You people have no taste.

Oh, oh behold that wondrous sight of divine light.
Lava lamp, you say?
We must base the room on it.

Suspend it from a blue nylon string.
Knock down this wall
And this one for the extra space.
Paint the rubble pink,
Totem pole here,
And they said I was mad.
And voila!
So, what do you think?

Antonia Russell-Clark (15)
The Mountbatten School

THE SUN WAS ONLY SLEEPING

Do not say it's over
It's not, and never was.
Repeat the drone with us.
We'll fight the battle as before.
So take my hand, I'll lead the way
Into a sunset dead.
In similar verse, day by day,
Our lives are led by silver thread.
Come forth with me, wake land and sea.
The sun was only sleeping.
A dawn will come, our lives aren't done,
Though we feel sorrow creeping.
Conduct the sea and guide the breeze
In their musical tale.
The repeated drone - not as before,
Is just the guiding bass.
Don't say it's alright - you know it's not.
How boring that would be -
To have a rest from life's spitefulness.
Sweet life goes on, ironically.

Rachel Whitworth (15)
The Mountbatten School